THE BIG CLEAN
HOW TO CLEAN AND ORGANIZE YOUR HOME AND FREE YOUR MIND
REVISED AND UPDATED

ALSO BY KIM RINEHART:

Goodbye, Fatty! Hello, Skinny! How I Lost Weight And Still Ate The Foods I Loved—Without Dieting

THE BIG CLEAN
HOW TO CLEAN AND ORGANIZE YOUR HOME AND FREE YOUR MIND
YOUR MIND
REVISED AND UPDATED

KIM RINEHART

ARTRUM MEDIA

For my sister's cats.

The Big Clean: How to Clean and Organize Your Home and Free Your Mind (Revised and Updated) Copyright © 2009 by Kim Rinehart.

Paperback ISBN-13: 978-0-9841957-4-9
Paperback ISBN-10: 0-9841957-4-2

Published by Artrum Media.

eBook ISBN–13: 978-0-9841957-5-6
eBook ISBN–10: 0-9841957-5-0

CONTENTS

IT'S NOT HARD—YOU CAN DO IT!

Don't you wish you had a maid? Wouldn't it be nice to come home to a clean house that's free of clutter? Wouldn't it be nice to see everything in its place and dust free? Wouldn't it be nice to see freshly vacuumed carpets and shiny wood floors? Wouldn't it be nice to have someone else do it for you?

Yeah, it would.

But, if you're like me, you can't afford a maid. However you still want a relatively clean house with the least amount of effort. Don't think it's possible? Well, I'm here to tell you that you can have it. It doesn't take much and once you start with a clean slate, i.e. by doing some deep cleaning and de-cluttering, all you have to do is maintain it.

It's called The Big Clean.

The Big Clean is a system I came up with that allows me to go for stretches of time without worrying about housework. I do a Big Clean for each room in my house about once a year. After that, the rest is cake. And after The Big Clean is done, all I generally have to do is put in thirty minutes or less a week to keep my house clean. And I can even do it in increments of five or ten minutes and not all at once.

So, why should you do this? I mean, what are the benefits of doing a deep clean and getting organized? Well, for one thing, wouldn't it be nice not to dread coming home? Knowing you can come home to a place that is clean and in order and where you can find stuff is the best feeling. It gives you a sense of control. Knowing that if you pick up a little here or wipe a little there—and that's all you have to do—your home will stay clean is a great feeling. It frees up your mind so you can concentrate on the more important things in life like dating or kids or shopping online.

I'm going to tell you how I do it. I'm going to take you step-by-step into the process that works best for me. Everyone that comes into my house tells me how clean it is and wants to know how I do it. It doesn't take that much. Sure, a few times a year I have to wash windows—and I *hate* washing windows—and clean the interior doors but other than that, it's pretty easy to maintain the clean. That is, once your home is clean and clear of clutter.

This should go without saying, but if you live in a huge house and not the standard three-bedroom, then it might take you a little longer to clean it. But don't worry. If you follow the advice in this book, you will still it get cleaned much more quickly than you would have otherwise.

The key to a clean house is organization. The great thing is it doesn't take much to organize your house. And by doing this, you will free up a lot of time which would otherwise be spent looking for a lost shoe or letter or whatever. You won't waste so much time shoving undesirables out of your way.

There are perks to getting organized:
- Free up time better spent crashing on the couch.
- More space in your house. *Ahh!* Breathe in the non-cluttered smell of freedom!
- You might just find out where that bad smell is coming from.
- Less stress getting ready in the morning, while cooking, or sleeping.
- Fewer stumped toes when moving around useless junk.

A good point to mention is that you don't have to tackle everything all at once or all in one day. Just start on the little stuff that is driving you batty, then build on that. Pick a day to do this room or that room, and then do it. And, yes, I said *room*, not drawer.

And when you're done, give yourself a little reward. (I'm talking about an ice cream cone or nice dinner out, not more junk to clutter your place up again.) Also, while you're doing it, try not to get too overwhelmed. If you start feeling a little caged in, simply take a breather and come back to it later. The important thing to do is to *actually come back and finish the work*. So, be diligent and once it's done, you will find yourself with a groovy, clean home that you will enjoy coming home to every single day. And that's the whole point, right? After you're finished, you might even like to invite some people over so they can enjoy it, too.

FESS UP TO THE MESS

We all know how to clean. Right? I would hope so. But for those of you who find that your house is a…well, a mess but don't know how to exactly get it clean, I am going to include a few tips along the way in order to help you understand how to get it tidy and *keep* it tidy.

As I said earlier, once your house is clean, it will be easier to keep it clean by doing little things every other day. Pick a day for laundry, a day for cleaning the bathroom, etc. Or you can save it all for one day. The choice is yours. Again, if it's really clean, all you're going to have to do for a month or so is spot clean.

Some people hate to clean house with a vengeance. My sister is one of those people. Besides that, she has three cats. Let's just leave it at that. However, even if you hate to clean house like my sister, by following this system of cleaning, you can maintain a relatively clean home.

It shouldn't take much to convince you that there is nothing like a clean home. I just love to look around mine. Maybe that makes me anal-retentive or a type-A personality, but, hey, I like to touch things without having my fingers stick to them.

But before we get to all that, you need to survey your house and figure out just what you're up against. Go ahead, take a look around. Are there magazines and newspapers everywhere? Is there a mountain of dirty towels in the bathroom? Does everything seem to have a slightly nasty film over it? Does it look like someone had a party and forgot to invite you but you still have to clean up the mess?

Is it that bad? If so, don't freak out. Take a few deep, cleansing breaths. It's not as bad as it looks. Well, maybe it is. Nevertheless, it's time to fess up to the mess your home is in and own it. Yeah, just like all those talk-show hosts are always telling people to own their problems, you have to own your dirty house and then you can do something about it.

It's easy, at first, to get overwhelmed. Instead of doing that, start with one thing and then move to the next. This doesn't have to be done in one day. You'll be breaking up big tasks into several smaller, more manageable ones. Tackle one job—like dusting—all at once, then move on to the next project. That way, if you get fed up with it and don't want to do anymore, at least that part is done.

So, take a look around your home. It might look worse than it is. I know it's hard to start a cleaning frenzy when everything is out of order and dirty. But the trick is to start slow. And then do it and get it over so you can have some time for *yourself.*

Important note: Always, always wear old clothes when you are cleaning. You will ruin a nice outfit if you don't watch it.

Another important thing to do: Open a window as you're cleaning because the fumes from cleaning products can and will make you sick. I'll say this occasionally throughout the book just to remind you.

One last important note: It might be a good idea to wear some safety goggles as you clean. Spraying cleaners onto surfaces can come back squirt into your eyes. You can get a lightweight pair just about anywhere.

With all that said and done, let's go through a few basic cleaning tasks.

BASIC CLEANING 101:

- How to clean coffee maker: Get a bottle of vinegar and pour into coffee pot—or carafe or whatever you call it—until it's about ¼ full. Now pour in some water until it's almost full. Pour into coffee maker and turn it on. Once this mixture has run through the maker, empty it out and fill the pot with water. Pour into maker and run it though. The vinegar will take out the grit from the coffee maker and your coffee will taste fresher. After that's done, you can wash out the pot in the sink with dishwashing liquid and then wipe down the maker with Windex or just a hot rag.

- Cleaning wood tables: It is best to clean wood tables with furniture polish or lemon oil. It's also a good idea to clean with an old rag instead of paper towels because paper towels leave little traces of lint. Be sure to clean the legs as well and don't overuse the cleaner because you don't want excess oil on your tables. Just enough to lift the dust and give a little gleam.

- Wood spindles on the stairs: Every once in a while, clean each spindle with lemon oil and an old rag. It's greasy but your spindles will shine. Also, the wood will soak up the oil. If you have painted spindles, just wipe them with a slightly damp cloth or a cleaner like Fantastic. (Be sure to test an inconspicuous spot to make sure it doesn't strip any paint off.)

- Wood floor: It's best to mop a wood floor with oil soap, like Murphy's or with plain warm water. If you have laminate floors, it is best to use mop with water as most cleaners can make them streak.

- Tile or linoleum floor: Get a bucket and fill it with hot water then pour a little bleach into it. This will make the floor sparkle. However, if you are afraid of stripping the finish, use something like Mop&Glo.

- Computer screen: You can get cleaning cloths designed specially to clean the screen just about anywhere. Some people use a water and alcohol solution—35% alcohol, 65% water—but I find the cloths work better. You can also buy a thick painter's brush at an art store to dust the key board and the tower.
- TV: Clean with Windex and paper towels. Be sure to turn it off first! If you have an LCD or plasma screen, follow manufacture's instructions, otherwise you can clean with a soft cloth or a duster from Swiffer.
- Kitchen counter: Depending on the surface, you can usually clean with a little bleach water. You can also make your own: Get an empty spray bottle and put in one part bleach and ten parts water.
- Faucets: Clean with Windex or a non-abrasive spray like a soap scum remover.
- Bathroom sinks: Use Comet or Scrubbing Bubbles.
- Microwave: Fill a bowl with water and put it in there. Turn it on until it boils. The water will splash everywhere and take off any caked-on food. Open, remove bowl with an oven mitt, then wipe clean with a paper towel. Or you can just use a degreaser.
- Dishwasher: Run an empty load with a little bleach. This will sanitize your dishwasher. For every third or fourth load, I pour a little bleach in with my dishes to sanitize them as well.
- Miscellaneous stuff: Like the things in the bottom of the sink that catch food, your scrub brushes and the drip pans on your stove can be thrown into the dishwasher from time to time to decontaminate.
- Lamps: Can be vacuumed off with a hand-vac. (More on that later.)
- Rugs: Every home needs a rug at every door that leads to the outside. This catches all kinds of dirt. To clean, run vacuum cleaner over and about every two months

or so, throw them in the washer unless they are wool which, in that case, just vacuum. Note: Always buy rugs with foam backs—or buy a non-skid rug pad—so they don't slide all over the place. This can be a potential hazard and we wouldn't want you to get hurt over a silly rug.

- Smooth surface stove: Everyone knows that it's hard to get gunk up off these things, but I have found that using a magic eraser, like Mr. Clean, is the best way. Simply run the eraser under the tap, squeeze out excess water and then clean the top. It's worked for me every time. Follow with a multi-purpose cleaner for shine or Windex.

Now let's talk about things that need to be done around the house from time to time. These things can be done once or twice a year, depending how dirty and cluttered they get. Note that this is just a general list and may not include everything in your home that needs cleaning. The point is to get yourself in the mindset of things that should be done within this amount of time.

About once or twice a year:
- Wash windows.
- Steam clean carpets.
- Clean baseboards and tops of door frames. (Or use the attachment on a vacuum and run over to get accumulated dust. If there's grim, just wash with a rag.)
- Clean the kitchen cabinets out, including the top.
- Clean out closets, vanities, medicine cabinets, dressers, etc.
- Sort all financial papers and then shred what you don't need anymore.
- Clean overhead fixtures and ceiling fans.
- Remove cobwebs from walls and ceilings.

- Clean refrigerator and freezer. (Always check expiration dates on food and throw out any out of date items.)
- Clean coffee pot. (As described above.)
- Go through all bookshelves and de-clutter and dust.

That doesn't look so bad, does it? Nope. Let's move on.

A COUPLE OF HOURS

Depending on the size of the rooms in your home, it should only take you a couple of hours per room to do the cleaning/de-cluttering. Of course, the bigger the room, the more it's going to suck your time. The kitchen will probably take the longest because it has more cabinets and the refrigerator.

However, it also depends on how fast you work. I work very fast so I can get it done and get on with my life. Work at your own pace and take breaks when necessary. But once you start a project, it's best to go ahead and finish it. Make a pact with yourself to finish it once you've started. Procrastination is no one's friend, so the sooner you start, the sooner you will be finished.

IF YOU CAN'T USE IT, CHUCK IT

Does your house look like *Sanford and Son* lives there? Come on, be honest.

The very first step to a clean house is getting rid of the junk that clutters it up. Most people have way too much clutter in their homes. I know I do and I throw junk out all the time.

Don't you sometimes wonder where this stuff comes from? I mean you pick it up and remember when you bought it and where it came from and how much it cost, but then you think, "What am I? Stupid? This is a piece of crap!"

It's time to get rid of it.

Let's go through your house, shall we? What a mess, huh? I go through my house about twice a year and get rid of a lot of junk. Usually I just donate all my old junk unless I've paid a lot of money for it, then I try to find somewhere to sell it. However, if I can't sell it, I donate it.

Again, this will probably take a few hours, so pick your day and send everyone away. If you're married, be warned that if you throw some of "*his*" junk away, you might have a big fight on your hands. (I sneak and do it all the time and *always* get busted!) So, to avoid those messy fights, make a pile of his junk and ask/demand him to go through it. If he refuses, threaten to throw it away. He'll step to it.

Ready?

Start slow when de-cluttering. Go room by room. For instance, start in the bathroom and any shampoo or hairbrush you don't need, chuck it. We'll get more into detail a little later on as we are going to go through every single room in your house and clean/de-clutter it, but right now, start slow.

What you need to do is to set a goal of one room a day and if you can't swing that because of kids or your work schedule, one room a week. You can enlist people to help, but I know if I do this when my husband is around, he'll say, "Why are you getting rid of that?! Give it back!" And then I have to take time to tell him off.

Once you have all the junk that you want to dispose of, make a point to dispose of it.

PLACES WHERE YOU CAN GET RID OF YOUR OLD STUFF:

- Charity shops like Goodwill and Salvation Army. Sometimes, if you have big items like a sofa or TV, they will pick them up. Just call and ask. If not, you might have to take it yourself. A perk of doing this is that you can ask for a receipt and take the donation off your taxes. (However, be sure to check with your accountant first if this is your intention.)

- Any online auction place like Ebay or Yahoo! Auctions. You need to be aware that you will have to take a picture of the item with a digital camera, and then upload it and the information about the product. You will also have to get a Paypal account. If you have a lot of stuff like vintage clothing to sell, however, it might be worth the effort. But go in knowing that it can be a lot of work. And don't forget, you'll have to pack and ship the items as well, so be sure to include a shipping price on your listing.

- Yard sales are a great way to get rid of junk. I have included a whole chapter at the end to let you know what's involved. And, yes, it's a lot of work. But if you have a lot of stuff, you might be able to make some money.

- Consignment shops are also a great way to dispose of your old clothes, purses and shoes for cash. Again, I have a whole chapter devoted to this one.
- Relatives or neighbors might come by your place and take all your old junk off your hands, especially if they're the type who likes free stuff. Just an idea.

If you have stuff you might like to keep, find a room in your house where you can store it so that it doesn't take up as much room. If you don't have a room, find a closet or an outside building or an attic, just so it's no longer in your way.

If you find that you have so much junk that you can't store it in your home, then either rent some storage space or go through it again and give what you can away until it becomes more manageable.

On the other hand, if you have a lot of stuff you're keeping because of an emotional attachment, why not take a picture or video it? That way, you can still have the memory but not so much clutter.

Now once you've stored it, wait a month or two and, if you haven't gone in there and gotten it out, either have a yard sale or give it to charity. If you haven't used it in by then, more than likely, you never will. And it's time to go. Chances are, you'll ask yourself why you kept it to begin with.

HERE'S HOW IT WORKS:
- If you can't use it, chuck it.
- Set a goal of one room per week to de-clutter until you've done all rooms.
- If you think you have to keep something, put it in a closet or a room and wait a few months. If you don't miss it, you don't need it. If you find yourself looking for it, keep it. If not, out it goes.

- If you still don't have space for something but have an emotional attachment, why not take a picture or video it and then get rid of it?
- There are lots of ways to get rid of junk including donating to worthwhile charities.

YOUR PURSE

If you're a woman, the first step to an organized home and an organized life is an organized purse. I find nothing in the world more frustrating than looking for something in my purse and having to pull out all kinds of junk. There's usually a crowd around when I do this, too. It's embarrassing, to say the least.

HERE'S WHAT YOU DO:

- Clear off the kitchen table, hold your purse upside down and shake everything out of it.
- Make sure the stuff in the little zippered pockets is out, too.
- Take your purse to the trash can, hold it upside down and shake it out again. (Make sure that you get all the dust and bread crumbs out.)
- Go back to the table and begin to sort through the junk.
- Make three piles: One to keep, one to store and one to chuck. Keep sorting until you have it done.
- Once you're done, put the stuff you need back in and put all the other stuff where it goes. (Barrettes into the bathroom, bills where they go, etc.)
- Done!
- Do the same thing for your wallet and cosmetic case, if you have one.

Big, fat important note: Take all the contents of your wallet and photocopy every single item—front and back. This includes your driver's license, your social security card, your credit cards—everything that is important. That way, if your purse is lost or stolen, you already have the information. It's also important to note that you need to keep this somewhere you can find it. So don't just copy it and forget about it. *Put it somewhere where you can find it.*

(And don't put it in your purse because that defeats the purpose.)

Another good thing to do is to get an address book and write down all those addresses that are floating around your purse and home. If you have a lot of business cards, get some clear tape and just tape them in there. This saves tons of time when you need to get in touch with someone.

HERE'S HOW IT WORKS:

- Begin organizing your life by organizing your purse.
- Once you've done that, take all the important contents of your wallet and photocopy them.
- Get an address book and write down all those numbers floating around at the bottom of your purse. You can just tape the business cards in there, if you like.

BUY A JEWELRY BOX...OR, ER, THING

If you don't already have a jewelry box, get one. A nice one *without* a little pink ballerina is preferable. But if you've got so much stuff that you need to buy a chest to put all of it in, then you've got way too much stuff and that means it's time to go through it and get rid of some of it. Even if it means selling it online. No one needs that much jewelry except the Queen and she's got a room to store her stuff in. And a few guards.

I have a big red leather jewelry box that has a few drawers. Yours can be smaller or bigger or whatever. You don't even *have* to buy a jewelry box. You can buy a silver bowl or a basket or whatever catches your eye. Having a jewelry—let's call it a thing—*thing* is going to save you so much time and probably money. That way, you pull your jewelry off at the end of the day, throw it in your thing and when you go look for it, there it will be.

What a concept.

HERE'S HOW IT WORKS:
- Buy something nice to put all your jewelry in, whether it's a box or a nice bowl or whatever.
- When you pull your jewelry off, you can just toss it in the box and won't have to worry about where it's gotten off to.

THOSE DUST BUNNIES HAVE MET THEIR MATCH!

I think I am obsessed with vacuum cleaners. I have bought three in the last few years: A big upright, a small hand-vac and one just to clean the wood floors in my house. And the reason I need so many vacuum cleaners? Because they catch dust bunnies like nobody's business. Also, I'm always looking for a bigger, better one.

Vacuum cleaners are dust suckers. They are also the best things to get your house clean of dust. It saves time and money on furniture polish and feather dusters. Also, I don't have to shake out my area rugs all the time. I just go from hardwood to carpet in two shakes of a lamb's tale. I also dust with a vacuum cleaner. Yup, you heard me.

The most important vacuum cleaner in my house is my hand-vac. Forget lemon oil and dusting cloths and your hands getting greasy using the stuff. Do what I do and just buy a small hand-vac and dust everything in your house with it.

Here's the kind of hand-vac you need:
- Buy an electric hand-vac or a really good rechargeable one. The good rechargeable kinds will set you back a few dollars but are more than worth it. However, if you don't want to spend the extra cash, get a good electric one.
- Buy one that has an attachable hose to get in smaller crevices.
- The smaller the vac, the better. Smaller means less weight so your arms won't tire out as much.

I take my little vac out and dust all surfaces with it. It sucks the dust right up. The best thing about this is that no dust clouds form as I'm doing it, which means I'm not redistributing the dust to another area of my home. And I don't end up sneezing my head off.

You can dust all kinds of stuff with it:
- Knickknacks.
- The couch.
- The commode. (Yeah, dust forms on the top.)
- The stereo.
- The TV.
- The plants.
- The kitchen counter.
- Just about anything and everywhere.

I have a friend who dusts her cats with her hand-vac. And she says the cats love it and she doesn't have to worry about stray hairs everywhere.

Now onto the upright vacuum. If you don't have a good upright vacuum cleaner, if at all possible, invest in one. This thing is going to save you so much time it's unbelievable. When you buy one, keep in mind that the ones with an "easy empty" dirt container are the best. All you have to do is empty it out into the garbage can. Besides, who wants to worry about what size vacuum bag to buy? I don't.

You can use your upright vacuum on all surfaces:
- Carpet.
- Tile.
- Linoleum.
- Hardwood floors.
- Mattress. (To suck all the dust and dust mites out of your bed.)

It is the best way to go. Once you try it, you will be hooked. It's quick, it's easy and it's efficient. Those dust bunnies have met their match.

I have also found that those thick artist's brushes are great to clean things like the computer keyboard and the vents in the car. You can use them in any teeny-tiny spaces that gather dust where you can't go with your hand-vac. Once you're done, take your hand-vac and dust off the tips of the brushes. Dust's gone for good!

HERE'S HOW IT WORKS:

- Get yourself a hand-vac and dust everything in your house. This sucks the dust right up and you're not redistributing it from one part of the house to the other.
- Use your upright on all floor surfaces.
- Get a few artists' brushes to get into tiny crevices like computer keyboards.

"MAKE YOUR LIFE EASIER?" YEAH RIGHT!

How much money have you spent buying all kinds of products that are supposed to "make your life easier"? The next question is: How many actually worked?

If you're like me, you've spent a lot of money on these things that give hollow promises. Stop doing it today and save your money for the future. I once paid almost forty bucks for a "steam" iron that could "steam" out wrinkles. It was the answer to all my problems! No more ironing! If only... Of course, it did not work at all. Forty bucks down the drain for a piece of junk I ended up giving to charity.

I know some companies offer a "money-back" guarantee. And they do that because they know most of us aren't going to take the time to put it back in the box, address it, and write a letter asking for our money back. I never do, anyway.

But then you think, "It's only forty dollars." Forty dollars is a good meal out at a nice restaurant. It's dinner and a movie! It's gas for your car or it's money you could save for a nice vacation or a massage. You need that forty bucks more than they do, believe me.

I'll tell you how to make your life easier. Stop wasting money on this junk that never works. I did. I just started saying no to infomercials. Whenever they come on and try to draw me in, I turn the channel.

You only need the basic stuff to clean with. You don't need any "wonder" product. And what's going to get your house clean is mostly elbow grease anyway. Besides that, it burns calories and uses your muscles.

There are no quick fixes to cleaning a house and no product out there is going to help you do it any better or any easier or any faster. Sure, some good products come along occasionally that make things easier, but remember to use judgment. If it seems too good to be true, then it probably is.

If you have to keep "replacing" cloths for that handy sweeper thing, factor in how much money you're spending. Sometimes you can get a broom and a dust pan for two bucks. What if you run out of the cloths when you need to clean? You're going to have to clean with a broom and a mop, that's what.

Instead of always buying a gazillion sponges, just use your old washcloths. Besides the fact that they don't harbor all kinds of harmful bacteria like sponges do, they are the best things to clean with. With a little cleaner, old washcloths work twice as good as a sponge and you can use them for dusting, cleaning the bathroom *and* the kitchen. It also saves on the paper towels. In addition to that, all you have to do is throw them in the washer once you're done cleaning with them. Just use a little bleach and they're good to go in no time flat.

BASIC CLEANING MATERIALS NEEDED:
- One broom.
- One mop.
- One vacuum cleaner.
- One hand-vac.
- Some old rags/washcloths.
- A bucket.
- Some paper towels.
- Toilet bowl cleaner like Comet or Lysol.
- Some bleach and/or cleaning spray.
- A few small scrubber brushes.

That's it. You don't need anything fancy or that costs lots of money.

Look at it this way: A good old mop isn't going to be updated and improved because it's pretty much perfect on its own. But if you like spending that extra money and wasting your time trying to figure out some new gadget then go for it.

HERE'S HOW IT WORKS:

- You don't need any fancy gadget to clean with.
- Fancy gadgets aren't going to make the task of cleaning any easier or any quicker.
- Use your old washcloths to clean with instead of sponges. (Sponges are breeding ground for all kinds of bacteria.)
- Buy the basic things you need and they will last you a long time. In addition to that, they will save you a lot of money.

MULTI-TASK YOUR LAUNDRY

Before you start your cleaning frenzy, grab a load of laundry and get that going as you're cleaning. When it finishes, go put it in the dryer and start another load. This way, it's done when you are and you can fold your clothes and then kick back and watch some TV. Because you'll be done for the week.

Caution: Do not ever leave home with your dryer going. It is a fire hazard! And always, always, clean out the lint filter. *Always!* You can get a little trash can for your laundry room so you can easily dispose of the lint that comes out of the dryer filter. It wouldn't hurt to take your hand-vac every once in a while and dust out the lint hole and filter. Also, if you can swing it, the back of your dryer needs to be vacuumed, along with the tube that goes outside. Just do this occasionally.

Note: Don't try to move your dryer by yourself or you will end up with a pulled muscle. Get someone to help you do this.

If you have to go to a Laundromat to do your laundry, I feel for you, I really, really do. (I know I used to have to do this and it drove me insane.) I wouldn't suggest taking your laundry there and leaving it as people can steal your clothes. Instead, just take it over there and get it done.

HERE'S HOW IT WORKS:
- As you're cleaning, throw a load of laundry into the wash and when you're done, it will be done, too.
- Clean out your lint filter and vacuum around the lint hole from time to time.
- Never leave your house with your dryer going. It's a fire hazard.

YOUR CLOSET HAS MET ITS MATCH

Your closet. I can just imagine how overstuffed that thing is. You might even have a few critters living in there! You'd never know because you can't see anything. And if you can't see anything that means you can't *find* anything.

I'm just kidding about the critters, but if you're like most women, you've got a little too much in there, don't you? You know you don't need it. You're not going to wear it. And I'd be willing to bet, a lot of it is out of style. No one wants to be "so last season," do they? I know I don't.

I think that once you get your closet organized, you will see how easy it will be to tackle all the other tasks in your home. Also, it's so nice to open the closet door and be able to see what's in there. You can breathe easy. You can find your shoes! You can get dressed in no time flat.

Another good thing about doing this is that you can also make some cash. Yup, that's right. I have made a small fortune by selling my old clothes at consignment stores. Of course, I don't factor in how much I actually spent on this stuff in the first place. But then again, what good is the stuff if it's just hanging in my closet? Nada. (We'll go into detail about that in the next chapter.)

Okay, if you're like my friend—let's call her Sandy—you are probably shaking in your shoes thinking about that mess you call your closet. Her closet is so jam-packed if you removed one single item, the whole thing would fall apart and crash on your head.

But she did it and so can you.

Take a day and promise yourself you are going to do it. Send everyone out of the house and do it alone. You don't want your friends hanging around going, "How cute! Can I have it?!" No, they can't have it. You're selling it. You need this money to buy some new stuff.

SUPPLIES YOU WILL NEED FOR THIS TASK:

- A hand-vac.
- Plastic hangers. (The more, the better.)
- A few garment bags. (Optional.)
- A few garbage bags for the charity pile.
- A few shopping bags for the consignment pile stuff to put in purses and shoes. (I always save my big shopping bags from the mall just for this task.)
- Clear, plastic shoe boxes. (Optional.)

Ready?

Approach your closet like a bull in a china shop and tear the mother apart. Don't just sort through the stuff as this will not work. Yank it all out, throw it on the floor and go in for another bunch.

Yes, you heard me right. Empty it all out. Now. *Go!*

When you've emptied the whole thing out, sit down and ask yourself how you got into this mess to begin with. Once you've answered to the best of your ability, go get your vacuum cleaner. Using your nifty hand-vac, vacuum every square inch of that closet. (You will not believe the cobwebs you will find.) Vacuum the floor and the ceiling even if you have to go get the stepstool or a *sturdy* chair. Clean it good from top to bottom and then take a look at that mess on the floor.

Now step to it. Make three piles. One pile for consignment and one for charity. One pile to keep.

Let's do this one more time. Three piles:

- One for consignment.
- One for charity.
- One to keep.

This is the most important thing you are ever going to hear, so listen closely: *You should only keep what you know you are going to wear.* Do I have to say it again for good measure? I will. I don't mind. *You should only keep what you know you are going to wear.*

Have you gotten that through your head yet? I know that this little outfit means this and that sweater means that, so take a few pictures of your favorite items and then chuck them. You will thank me later for this. Believe me.

Good.

Now it's time to try on everything that you've decided to keep. Sometimes, it might not fit the way you remember. You could have lost or gained a little weight and that means it's taking up precious space. If so, get rid of it. If you're keeping any jeans or relics from your high school days in hopes that you might lose weight and be able to wear them again, keep in mind that they will be out of style. The cut and fit of jeans *always* change. So, throw out that old junk and promise to buy a new pair of jeans.

Also, do not keep anything under the pretense that it will "come back in fashion." Even stuff that comes back into style from yesteryear has been updated and tweaked when it comes back around. Of course, if you have something you love, don't throw it out just to make room. But if you get no use out of it, why keep it? (This doesn't apply to things like wedding dresses or your baby shoes, of course. But if you have five bride's maid's dresses... Well, what are you keeping them for?)

On with the show...

Start picking up items, examine them and ask yourself what the heck you were thinking. "Here we have a lime green turtleneck no one in their right mind would ever wear..." Something like that should go into the charity pile.

THE CHARITY PILE:

- Anything over two years old.
- Anything that has rips or tears or stains.
- Anything that is "pilling"—little fuzzies all over it, especially at the neck and collar.
- Anything that has lost its shape, like sweaters.
- Anything that needs to be "fixed"—needs buttons sewed, pants or skirts hemmed or any other mending. (I usually just get rid of it. I hate to sew buttons or hem pants and skirts and I also hate to find someone to do it for me. It's your choice, though. If you want to promise yourself that you'll get it fixed, put it back in the closet and next time you clean it out, you can promise again. History does repeat itself.)

QUESTIONS TO ASK WHEN SORTING CLOTHES:

- How old is thing?
- What does it go with?
- Double knit polyester will never come back in style, will it? (No!)
- When was the last time I wore it?
- Did I even like it in the first place?
- How does it look on me? Good rule of thumb: If anything makes your butt look big, throw it out! Make sure it is comfortable, doesn't bunch up or go up your butt. Does the stitching creak when you hug yourself or bend at the knees? Do the pants legs cover your feet? If they're not Capri's, then get rid of them.
- Is it high maintenance? Does it have to be dry cleaned, laid flat to dry, hand-washed or any other pain in the butt thing? Get rid of it if so. (Unless, of course, you like doing lots of extra work or it's a fabulous cashmere sweater.)
- Does this shirt (or pants or whatever) look just like *that* one? (Funny story. I once found the *perfect* pair of jeans

that I never wore. I put them up and completely forgot about them. A few months later, I bought the exact same pair on sale! And after that, I found the original pair.)

Only keep stuff you know you will wear. Don't fool yourself into thinking you'll wear it "when you lose weight" or "when you are asked to a ball" or "when disco comes back in." (I know disco has been back in style forever but those pants sure ain't.)

One more thing. You should keep a nice dress or outfit around to wear to funerals or big functions. I call this my "serious outfit." If you don't have one, put it on your list of things to buy in the future. You can spend a little extra on this, but be sure to buy something basic—preferably in black—that will last years.

THE CONSIGNMENT PILE:
- Anything you don't want that is none of the aforementioned.
- Leather jackets you no longer want, unless they are totally worn out.
- Leather pants. I mean, if you have a pair.
- Good jeans that are not too worn out. (One way to check is to look at the crotch. If the lining is ripping or wearing, throw those in the charity pile.)
- Sweaters that aren't bent out of shape.
- Shirts, skirts, pants that are in style.
- T-shirts that aren't too worn out.
- Purses and shoes that are in good shape and not out of style.

Okay, once you have the closet under control, go to your dresser, chest of drawers, lingerie chest, whatever. Get busy and do the same thing by emptying it out. Throw everything into piles, including bras and underwear. (You can donate old bras. Old underwear *can* be donated but I would suggest just throwing it out unless it's never been worn. Never send old underwear to consignment! The owner will look at you like you're crazy. This also goes for bathing suits unless they have never been worn and still have the tags on them.)

One thing that has saved me an enormous amount of time is the tall craft organizer thingamajig I bought in white and stuck it in a corner of my closet. It has seven drawers and in each, I have my various types of underclothes: Black bras in one, white bras in another, sports bras in yet another and the same goes with my panties. The bottom drawer is larger, so I have all my swimsuits in it. It's been a really handy thing to do and cost a little over a hundred bucks. If you have the cash, it's a worthwhile investment. Also, you wouldn't believe the time it saves not having to look for my favorite white bra. I also have a separate sock drawer.

Once you have this done, go through all the other closets in your place. Take out all old coats, shoes, anything that can be worn and put it in the piles. Handbags are always a hot item in consignment shops given that they are in good condition and are not falling apart. If they are, give them to charity or throw them out.

A few notes: If any pair of your pantyhose has "runs" in it, ditch it. If you have only one sock and the other has run away from home, throw it into the garbage. As soon as you get rid of it, the other one will return home to find himself getting dumped, too.

Now for your shoes. (By the way, how many pairs do you need?! I need a lot!) What's not going to consignment can be stored well. My suggestion is to buy some of those clear plastic shoe boxes to put them in. It keeps dust off and because its clear plastic, all you have to do is pick it up and look inside without popping the lid. They cost about a dollar each and you can get then just about anywhere. You can stack these neatly on the floor or if you have a big enough closet, buy a shelf and stack them on it. It can be a short shelf or a tall one. And the shelf doesn't have cost much. You can get cheap ones sometimes for thirty bucks and they work just as well as those ultra-expensive shoe caddies, which always seem to tear up.

If you do all this and still don't have enough room for everything, you can get some under-bed storage things. But my motto is: If I have to store it, I don't need it. But, of course, if you live in a smaller home, this may be the only option.

A good rule of thumb is this: Whenever you buy something new, eighty-six something old. (It's probably out of style anyway.) If it can go to consignment, have a part of your closet designated for it. The pile will increase in no time. Just don't leave it there. Make time to take it to the shop.

Buy some plastic garment bags to put your "serious outfits" in. That way, they won't get dusty hanging in your closet. I always shove these to the back of the closet so they're not in my way all the time.

On the top shelf of your closet, you can fold and store your jeans if you don't have enough room to hang them up. Just stack them on top of each other. You can do this with sweaters, too.

One thing I have in my closet is a basket where I throw all of my barrettes and pony-tail holders. That way, I just go to the basket, look around for the one I want and get going on my way.

You can also have a basket like this for all the other little things like belts. If you have room, I suggest you get one of those tie holders you can put on the wall. They're pegged and are perfect for hanging belts and scarves. Never hang belts or scarves on hangers because they always fall down and that means you always have to bend over and pick them up a gazillion times.

Now take a break. Get a soda and a cookie. Heck, get a drink of you need to. This is hard work, isn't it? Take a sip and breathe. Give yourself about five minutes of rest and head back in.

Oh, boy! You've got a horrendous mess! Time to clean it up.

Now that you have your three piles, you need to again try on *everything* that you want to keep. And I mean everything. Bras, underwear, coats, shoes, everything. Model in front of a mirror. How does it look? Have you ever worn it before? (Sometimes I find items that still have the tags on them.) Most importantly, *will you ever wear it again?* If not, chuck it.

Now look at your hangers. Are they from dry cleaners and made of metal? Do yourself a favor and throw out all those wire hangers before Joan Crawford comes over. In addition to pissing her off, they will ruin your clothes by bending and rusting. Besides that, they just look plain tacky. You can get a dozen or so plastic hangers for about a buck, which makes them cheaper than eggs. I buy all of mine in white because white always looks good with everything. (No, I am not anal-retentive, I swear!) Buy a few dozen. You can always use them and it's a pain in the butt to need a hanger and not have one.

After you have tried on all of your clothes—and probably have rediscovered some things you forgot you had—it's time to put *the things you want to keep* back into the closet and/or drawers. Hang everything that can be hung and fold everything neatly. It looks good now, doesn't it? You will find that you have so much more room and everything seems more spacious and nice. Good for you.

Now, look at those two remaining piles on the floor. Grab some garbage bags and put everything for charity into them, stick them into your car and find the donation center of your choice. Most towns have a Goodwill kiosk where you can donate at any time of the day. Find it and get rid of all that junk. Do it now. Don't wait. If you wait, then it will pile up and laugh at you every time you pass it. Take the time to do it now. *Phew.* That feels better when it's over.

And you're done with your closet! Pat yourself on the back and let's get going to the rest of your house. But first, you need to get your consignment stuff ready.

HERE'S HOW IT WORKS:

- Attack your closet like a bull in a China shop.
- Make three piles on the floor: One for charity, one for consignment, one to keep.
- Sort through everything and, once you've decided what you'd like to keep, try it on, even panties and bras.
- Once you're done with that, put all your clothes back into the closet on plastic hangers.
- Go through your dresser or any other place where you might have clothing and sort through it as well.
- Buy some plastic shoe boxes to put all your shoes in. (Keeps dust off.)
- Get a few garment bags to put your "serious" outfits in. (Ditto.)
- Go through all other closets in your house looking for clothing items you can either sell at consignment or give to charity.
- Buy a few baskets to store items like belts, scarves, hair accessories.
- Take all your charity items to charity ASAP. Don't let it sit around for weeks or you'll end up keeping it.

CH-CHING!

Now that your closet is nice and neat, you might be thinking of going the consignment route. If so, there are a few things to keep in mind and a few things to do before you go.

SUPPLIES YOU WILL NEED:
- Hangers. (You can use your old wire hangers, if you like, or buy a few plastic ones.)
- A few big shopping bags.
- Odor neutralizer like Febreze.

Note: You might be tempted to keep your clothes to sell at a yard sale but you need to know that clothes don't really sell well at yard sales. And if they do, you will probably have to end up selling them for a quarter. (And if you've spent a pretty penny or a pair of jeans or a sweater, this will really end up bugging you.) It's best to go ahead and take them to consignment or to charity. This way, you don't have to fold them neatly or buy one of those rolling hanger things to hang them on. Saves time and money.

First of all, you will have to sort through the pile. If anything needs to be laundered, wash it. If you have items that are dry clean only, don't spend the extra money to dry clean them in order to sell them. Check them over for dust and dirt and just shake them out. If you find a little dirt, get a wash cloth, wet the corner and wipe it off. (You can also use some odor neutralizer on them like Febreze.)

After that's done, hang all items on hangers. Now, go to your handbag, belt and shoe pile. Pick each item up and examine it. If anything is dusty, wipe it off. Put all of these items into a big bag.

Now you're ready to consign! Keep in mind that while it's not that hard to do, it is sometimes a pain in the butt. Ask yourself if you want to invest the time and if not, why not take all this stuff to charity? Your call. However, if you want to send your clothes to the consignment shop, here's the gist of it.

FAST FACTS ON HOW TO CONSIGN:

- Shops will only take items that are in season.
- Separate items into seasons: fall/winter; spring/summer. (This means no shorts in winter and no sweaters in summer.)
- After you've got your clothes separated into seasons, go to the phone book and find a consignment shop in the yellow pages.
- Call the shop and ask if they are accepting new items. Tell them what you have and when you can bring it in. (Some only take clothes by appointment, so *always* call first.)
- Be aware that most shops give you between 40-50 percent of what they actually sell the item for.
- If you want a certain price for an item—like a leather coat—tell them.
- Most shops pay once a month. Ask about this so you're not waiting in vain for your check. Even better, some shops will give you cash up front for your clothes when you bring them in. Ask to see if your consignment shop has this option. It's always better to get the money up front instead of waiting for months to get a check, in my opinion.
- Also, figure out if you want to pick up your check or just have it put in the mail. (There is *nothing* like getting a check in the mail when you least expect it.) So, tell the shop what you want to do.

- And, lastly, if your clothes don't sell, do you want to pick them up or have the shop donate them to charity? I always go the charity route, myself, as it's a pain to trek back to the shop and grab a big pile of clothes and bring it home. Besides, I don't want to find a space for this stuff.

If you have some vintage stuff, consider going the Ebay route or check around to see if your town has a vintage clothing shop. If so, call them and tell them you have some stuff you want to sell. (Most consignment shops I've dealt with don't sell that much vintage.) If the shop is interested in your stuff, they will probably just make you an offer and not consign it. Which means, you could leave with money in your pocket. *Ch-ching!*

That's pretty much it.

HERE'S HOW IT WORKS:

- Get your consignment items ready by laundering them.
- Hang everything on hangers.
- Put all shoes, belts and purses into a big bag.
- Call a shop and make arrangements to drop your stuff off.
- Ask about payment options—pick up check or have it mailed. Or, even better, ask about upfront cash.
- If you have vintage stuff, see if you can find a shop that specializes in this sort of thing. Or go the Ebay route.

HOW TO SAVE TIME IN THE MORNING

I know how tired you are from the workday. I know all you want to do is climb into bed and snuggle up and sleep. I also know you'd like to sleep in a little later the next morning. Am I right?

What I like to do is put my clothes out on a chair in my bedroom. I pre-pick my outfit, including shoes, socks, bra and all I have to do is put them on and I'm on my way after I finish my morning routine. And I get about twenty extra minutes of sleep every single day.

So if you can get it together, take a few minutes and grab your outfit. Sometimes I know you will have to try it on to make sure it looks good, so do that too. It will save you so much time it's unbelievable. And you might just be able to finish a dream every once in a while. In addition to that, it's easier to get your outfit ready when you're not still groggy from just waking up.

HERE'S HOW IT WORKS:
- Get your outfit for the next day ready before you go to bed.
- Sleep in and finish a dream every once in a while.

THE OTHER CLOSETS

How many other closets do you have? I only have three. And I thank the Lord everyday for this. I don't want any more than that. That's enough to keep up with.

SUPPLIES YOU WILL NEED FOR THIS TASK:
- A hand-vac.
- Hangers, preferably plastic.

Let's tackle the coat closet first, if you have one. Some call it the hall closet and some call it...something else. I call it the coat closet because that's where I keep all my coats, including winter, rain, sun, summer and spring. I let my husband keep his in there, as well.

This closet doesn't give me much trouble but it's about as big as a...umm, something *really* small. A grown human couldn't get in there. If your coat closet is bigger, I bet you've got bigger problems. And if you've got kids, even bigger problems. It's time to face this closet and move on with your life.

Let's get this over with painlessly and quickly:
- Go to that closet, fling open the door and duck!
- How much stuff just fell out of there? Kick it out of your way.
- Now pull *every single thing* out of that closet and take it somewhere like the living room where no one will trip over it.
- Get your nifty hand-vac and vacuum every square inch of that closet just like you did your other closet and clean it good.

- Go to that big mess you just threw in the middle of the living room floor.

Now let's begin the arduous task of sorting through your junk:

- Pick up each item and inspect it.
- Use the same line of thinking when you cleaned your clothes closet: Do you need it? Does anyone need it? If not, you know what to do. How long ago was it that you played *Clue?* If it's been over a year, chuck it.
- Place each item into piles of keep, consignment, charity and yard sale.
- Repeat until you have what you want to keep.
- Now take the pile that you don't want and put it in a garbage bag. You can store it somewhere if you're keeping it for the yard sale or you can just give it to charity. But if you don't intend on having a yard sale, give it away.
- Put your consignment items on hangers and take them to the shop ASAP.

The point of all this is to have a less cluttered, more organized closet. Go get some of your plastic hangers and put all the coats you are keeping back in there. Now look at the pile of all the other stuff on the floor you want to keep.

Divide it into categories:

- If it's a toy, make your kid put it up.
- If it's something for the car, put it in the car.
- And so and so forth.
- If it's not something that belongs in there, *don't put it back.* Find its correct place and then put it there.

Now, you're done for the day. Sit down and take a load off until it's time to tackle all the other closets. And then tackle them, one by one in the same manner as you did these first two until they are all cleaned out and de-cluttered.

Doesn't that feel so much better? You should be proud of what you've accomplished.

HERE'S HOW IT WORKS:

- Just attack all your other closets like you did your clothes closet.
- Put all items into piles: Charity, consignment, yard sale or keep.
- Find the correct place for each item and put it there.

YET ANOTHER ITTY-BITTY TIME-SAVER—BUYING IN BULK

I buy all of my toiletries and cleaning supplies in bulk not only because it's cheaper, but because I absolutely despise going into those gigantic super-savings centers any more than I have to. There is always so much noise and chaos going on it's a wonder anyone wants to shop there.

If you want to save time, pick a day and go to the gigantic store of your choice. Before you go, make a list of things you need. Go through your house and see what you're running low on. Then head off to the super-store in the sky, grab a cart and get going.

SOME RANDOM THINGS YOU MIGHT NEED IN BULK:
- Toilet paper.
- Paper towels. (I find that those that are "Select a Size" are the best around and you use less of them than the cheaper brands.)
- Cleaning supplies—at least two bottles of each.
- Laundry detergent, dryer sheets, bleach.
- Toothpaste, mouthwash, deodorant, etc.
- Dog/cat food.
- Sodas.
- Garbage bags.
- Light bulbs.
- Just about anything that doesn't expire within a year or so and you will eventually need.

This not only saves time, but it keeps you from having to go to the store in the middle of the week for toilet paper. Just be sure you have cleared a space to store this stuff.

WHAT'S IN THERE? THE LAUNDRY ROOM

Our next little project will be the laundry/utility room. It can also apply to the garage. If you don't have a laundry room or garage, proceed onto the next chapter. (However, you can apply these same principals to any room/closet you have that seems to accumulate all the odd stuff that doesn't go anywhere else.) If you do, sit down and let's get this over with as little pain as possible.

SUPPLIES YOU WILL NEED FOR THIS TASK:
- Hand-vac.
- Upright vacuum cleaner.
- A mop.
- A bucket.
- A washcloth.
- A broom.

For some reason, a wide variety of stuff that doesn't have anything to with the laundry or the car gets thrown into these rooms. When it gets to the point that you dread going in there, it's time to take action.

One of the best things you can do to find more space in these rooms is to install a few shelves. (You might already have cabinets and if so, you should consider yourself very lucky.) If you don't have room for any shelves, try to get those little stackable shelves and see if that saves room. You can stack them right on top of the other. But if you have room for more shelves, I suggest you get them. (You might have to have someone install them for you as you have to level the shelf and all that other manly stuff that makes my head hurt thinking about.)

I'll tell you how my laundry room looks but you can apply this to the garage as well.

Laundry room shelves:
- Two shelves above the washing machine and the dryer.
- On the top shelf, I put all of my bulk items like toilet paper and paper towels and light bulbs.
- The second shelf holds all of my cleaning products. I have my laundry detergent and my dryer sheets, a couple bottles of bleach and everything else that I need to clean with.
- On the other wall, I have a peg board that I bought in a home improvement store. I hang hats, my broom and mop and *anything* that can be hung up. (This saves so much room.)
- Above the peg board, I have another long shelf where I keep all the tools I own plus all that miscellaneous stuff like duct tape.
- Also, on this shelf, I have all of my tools in separate clear plastic shoe boxes that are labeled: Screwdriver, hammer, etc. So, when I need something, I know where it is. You can get a toolbox, but I find this to be much easier. Anything that's utilitarian goes in there.

If you have enough space in there, put your vacuum cleaner in the corner. Saves so much room and you always know where it's at.

Now it's time to tackle the room. And you can apply this same principal to the garage, as well.

HERE'S HOW YOU DO IT:
- Empty the entire room out, besides the washer and dryer and anything heavy like that in the garage.
- Once the room is empty, vacuum the top of the washing machine and dryer off then wipe them down with a wet washcloth.

- Run the broom along the top of the walls to get any cobwebs.
- Now mop the floor.
- Now go through all of your stuff and sort into piles: Keep, charity and garbage.
- Put all of your stuff back in there once you've sorted through it.
- Close the door and hope it stays nice and neat for a while.

There. That wasn't so bad, was it?

YOUR FINANCIAL HUB

Every well organized home needs a place for bill paying and other financial matters. That way, you're not always looking for a misplaced phone bill and you don't have to worry about your phone getting cut off.

This is one of the most grueling tasks I know of to getting de-cluttered and organized. I hate dealing with financial stuff. But I have to do it and it's time you do, too.

SUPPLIES YOU WILL NEED FOR THIS TASK:
- A hanging file box or a file cabinet. (You can also use shoe boxes, if you like.)
- A good electric shredder.
- Labels.

One of the most important things you can do is to designate a space where you can keep all of your financial records. If you don't have a home office and find that bills and other papers are lying around everywhere, you need to find a space where you can keep all this stuff under control. Designate a space in your house that will serve as your financial hub.

Your financial hub space could be:
- A corner of the kitchen counter. I have a wicker organizer that is used solely for my bills. This is where I keep my stamps, my savings book, my calculator, my checks and all bills that need to be paid. There are separate compartments for each. I go through it at least once a week to make sure everything has been paid on time.

- A corner in your bedroom, complete with a desk.
- A space in a closet—just install a few shelves. I have this plastic milk-crate thing that has hanging files in it. I paid ten bucks for it and stuck it in a closet. This is where I keep all my insurance papers, tax stuff and other financial papers.
- A filing cabinet stuck in the corner of just about any room.

It doesn't matter where you put it or what it is, as long as you put it somewhere. This space needs to be cleared of any other items not having to do with financial stuff.

Also, it doesn't matter what you buy to organize your financial stuff as long as you keep it separated. You can even use shoe boxes and label the outside of them: Bills to be paid, bills that are paid, insurance information, etc. You can stack the boxes on a shelf in a closet. The point is to get a filing system going so you can simplify your life and won't waste time looking for something important.

Once you've designated a space and have a filing system of some kind—shoe boxes, hanging folders, etc.—let's get on to the task of organizing your financial hub.

First off, go around your house collecting bills and other papers. Go through every drawer, every closet, or any other place where you might have some sort of papers. After you've gathered everything, it's time to organize it. *Piece by piece.* Don't just grab stuff and throw it into your files. Everything needs to be looked over. Pull everything out and as you're looking it over, place it in stacks as you go.

Separate things into three piles:
- One for stuff to keep.
- One for stuff to be paid.
- One for stuff to be thrown out/shredded.

Here is a guide to what you should keep and for how long. If you are confused about throwing *anything* out, call your bank or an accountant or another important person who knows about such things before you chuck it. The items I mention are the standard things you should keep. This is just a general guide and doesn't include every single piece of paper ever printed.

Keep these records for at least one year:
- Receipts.
- Utility bills.
- Check statements as well as savings statements.
- Insurance for car, health or any other kind.

Stuff you have to keep for at least seven years:
- All income tax records (You have to have this if you get audited—I hope and pray you never get audited.)
- Cancelled checks.
- Every document that supports your income tax record—cancelled checks, receipts, donations, etc.
- Contracts.
- Any cancelled checks that you've used for your tax records: mortgage interest, deductible items, etc.
- Anything to do with taxes *at all.*

Stuff you can never get rid of (and should be kept in a fire-proof safe):
- Birth certificate.
- Marriage license.
- Wills and trusts.
- Military papers.
- Contributions to an IRA
- Divorce papers. (Might be tempting to burn, but don't!)
- Passports.
- Social security cards. (You might not know this, but it's never a good idea to carry around your social security

card in case your wallet gets stolen. Just memorize it and put the actual card up somewhere safe.)
- Immigration papers.
- Visas.
- Any investment stuff.
- Home improvement stuff, i.e., receipts for any repairs you might have had done.
- Deeds or titles of any kind.
- Receipts or cancelled checks for payment of any sort of fine or traffic citation.

Now that you have your stacks in order, get your filing system down. For instance, if you buy hanging folders, label each one.

Hanging folders/filing cabinet:
- Bills to be paid.
- Insurance stuff.
- Taxes.
- Retirement accounts.
- And so on and so forth until you have all your papers in their proper place.

Use this system for any other system you might come up with, including using shoe boxes. It's also a good idea to get a few boxes and put all your old receipts, warranty information and owners manuals in. Just label the outside of the box and stick it in a closet.

Important note: *Anything that you no longer need that has any kind of personal information on it needs to be shredded, whether by hand or machine.* Do not ever throw anything in the garbage without doing this. There are people out there waiting for you to do it so they can steal your identity! Don't let them! Also, when you get offers for new credit cards in the mail, shred those as well. People can forge your name and have a good time on your good credit. It has happened to a lot of people and it can happen to you. Don't let it!

You can buy a good electric shredder for a little of nothing. They are worth their weight in gold. Just put it in a closet and plug it in when you get something you want to shred.

One last note…

Things you need at all times:
- Stamps. Keep a couple of books around at all times. (I always buy two when I have to go to the post office. Saves so much time!)
- Envelopes.
- Pens.
- A working calculator.

That should just about do it.

HERE'S HOW YOU DO IT:
- Designate a place in your home for your financial hub.
- Collect all bills and financial papers from around the house.
- Put it into three piles: Things that need to be paid, kept or thrown out.
- Label your filing system and put all papers in their proper place.
- Never throw anything out you're not sure of.
- Keep all important papers in a fire-proof box.
- Shred anything with any personal information on it. Note: When you get your credit card statement, make sure they don't send any of those checks. If they do, shred those as well instead of throwing them in the garbage.
- Get a few shoe boxes to put all of your receipts, warranties, and owner's manuals in.

COLLECTING IS FOR OLD WOMEN WITH BLUE HAIR— AND WEIRD MEN

I really do like my Aunt Louise but every time I go into her house, I get the heebie-jeebies. She has a glass menagerie that's just... It just makes my head hurt. She has so much junk! All those little knickknacks just sit around and collect dust. (Some of her little glass animals look creepy, too.)

Of course, anytime she shows me one of her new "pretties" I smile and say, "How cute!" I wouldn't hurt her feelings for the world but every once in a while I get the compulsion to grab a garbage bag and start throwing stuff in it.

I don't. For obvious reasons.

And we all know how some men collect comic books and baseball cards and little pieces of paper. This isn't collecting, people, it's hoarding. To me, it's just a little weird. Grown men with thousands of comic books... I... I don't know what to say. I know they're *valuable* but...

So what do you collect? I used to collect vintage alligator purses until I found myself with twenty and no room for the purses I actually *used*. Consider why you collect it and how much cash you're putting into it. Go from there. You *can* have too many ceramic frogs.

And get this: Less junk equals less dusting. It's true. I had about fifty or so picture frames all over my house. One day I couldn't take dusting the things one more time. I picked out my favorite pictures and left them. Then I took all the others out of their frames and put them in a really nice, leather photo album and got rid of most of the frames. Now I don't have to dust as much as I used to. Saves *so* much time.

If you can't part with your pretties why not buy a trunk and put it all in there? You still have it but it doesn't cause you extra work.

HERE'S HOW IT WORKS:
- Decide if you still want to invest in collecting.
- Less junk equals less dusting.
- If you can't part with your menagerie, why not get a trunk and put it in there so you won't have to dust it?

JUST A SUGGESTION FOR YOUR RECIPES

If you're like most of us, you have a ton of recipes floating around your kitchen. If you're like me, you're never going to make these delicious meals. And if you're like me, you don't want to get rid of any of your recipes just in case you're asked to make something spectacular one day.

So, how about getting a better system for your recipes?

A BETTER SYSTEM FOR RECIPES:
- Buy a photo album.
- Find all your recipes.
- Place all recipes into photo album and put it on a bookshelf or in one of your kitchen cabinets. (You can designate a space in a cabinet for this and all of your recipe books. Out of the way and dust doesn't settle on them. I find that the cabinet above the stove is the best place for this.)
- Or, you can laminate each recipe. That way, if and when you make it, it doesn't get stained.
- Laminated recipes can be kept in a nice recipe box that looks lovely on your kitchen counter or in the cabinet. (Or you can put them in a binder.)

Just a suggestion.

MOTH BE GONE!

Moths are the worst creatures in the whole world. They cause untold amounts of damage to beautiful things everywhere. For instance, I once found this gorgeous cashmere coat in a thrift store that had been eaten to almost shreds. I was so disappointed I wanted to cry. All because a moth got hungry. It's not fair!

You don't want this to happen to your clothes, believe me. But if you don't protect them from said moths, it will.

Moth balls smell horrendous but are a necessary evil. If you can't stand the smell, you can use cedar blocks or shavings instead. There are also several other products out now you can use in lieu of moth balls, like a product called Moth Away which is an herbal moth repellent. Any of these products can be used in the battle against moths. Just go to the store of your choice and select what you want to keep your clothes from being eaten.

Be sure to put the moth repellent in your closets and in your sweater drawer and anywhere a moth might feast. And if you see a moth in your house, do your best to get rid of him. He's out to destroy your clothes!

After a few months, you will need to check the moth repellent to make sure it's still active. A moth ball disintegrates and cedar blocks will need to be shaved to keep them active. Once mothballs are no longer active, you have to buy more. But it's a lot cheaper than buying new clothes.

HERE'S HOW IT WORKS:
- Buy moth repellent and put it anywhere a moth might have dinner.
- Be sure to replace every few months.

GREAT BIG GIGANTIC TIME-SAVER—STOP SORTING CLOTHES!

Get two laundry baskets. One for whites, one for colors. You'll never have to sort again. So much time saved!

If you have kids, then do the same thing for their closet. You can buy smaller laundry baskets and put them at the bottom of their closets. Then teach them how to do it. Kids are smart and they catch on quick. (Aren't you just waiting for the day when they can help with the dishes?)

HERE'S HOW IT WORKS:
- Buy two laundry baskets.
- One for white clothing.
- One for colored clothing.
- No need to spend time sorting clothes.

CH-CHING! MONEY-SAVER ALERT! RETURNS AND RECEIPTS

Whenever you buy *anything*, save your receipts. If you don't use it, return it and get your money back. But especially keep your receipts on the big ticket items like shoes and coats. You never know, you might buy it and leave it in the closet for all eternity.

Another thing, leave the tags on everything until the very day you're going to wear it. I always re-try everything on once I get home and if I don't like how I look in it in my own mirror, I take it back. And buy something better.

If you don't have time to return it because you're just too busy, put it back in the bag and throw it in your car—with receipt. When you find you're near the store, run in and get it over with.

I've returned waxing kits that didn't work and skin cream that broke me out and shirts I never wore and just about everything. Hey, they don't call it a money-back guarantee for nothing. *Take full advantage of this.* It's not like you're doing anything illegal or unethical by returning merchandise. Besides, if the store has a problem with a return, they will let you know that you can't return it.

HERE'S HOW IT WORKS:
- Save all receipts.
- Take everything back that you don't use or is defective.
- Put items into your car and when you go by the store, drop in and return.

IN THE KITCHEN

Okay, now that you have your closets in order and your financial hub…*humming*, it's time to move on to the bigger rooms. A good idea is to start in the kitchen. It always seems to be the messiest place in the house. The kitchen is one of the hardest rooms to clean because, well, that's where we cook. Pots and pans and dishes are everywhere, mostly in the sink. Bread crumbs are all over the counter. The stove is covered in grease and the refrigerator has a bottle of mustard in there from 2002.

Let's get started.

SUPPLIES YOU WILL NEED FOR THIS TASK:
- A hand-vac.
- An upright vacuum cleaner.
- A broom.
- A mop.
- A bucket.
- Some degreaser.
- A can of oven cleaner.
- Some Windex.
- Bleach.
- Oil soap if you have wood cabinets.
- Comet or, or if you prefer, a non-abrasive cleaner for the sink.

To begin with, there's not much you really need to cook with. Most of us have all sorts of things that we bought or were given that we don't need. Food processors, bread makers, two or three blenders, stuff like that. As you're cleaning out the kitchen, just go through all of this stuff in the same fashion as you did with your closets. There are a few universal things we all need, though.

But before you do anything, if you have any rugs in your kitchen, it's a good idea to throw them in the washer while all this is going on. If they're wool rugs, however, just move them out of the way until you've mopped, then replace and run them over with the vacuum.

THIS IS THE BASIC STUFF YOU NEED IN THE KITCHEN:

- Dishes. Buy a set that you like and can use for years.
- Good silverware. (No plastic spoons for you, young lady!)
- Good glasses that are thick and don't chip. And are stylish. These cost a little more but are worth the expense. (I have found that TJ Maxx occasionally gets in really good glasses that are a fraction of the cost of what they'd be at a department store like Saks.)
- A cutting board preferably made of plastic or glass because those wood ones become easily contaminated. (You can also stick it in the dishwasher after you've used it. Time-saver!)
- Spices. Just the basics that you will cook with: Oregano, garlic salt, hot sauce, etc. Don't buy any fancy ones on the premise that you're going to make a fancy meal. It's a waste of money and space. (If you want fancy spices, wait until you actually need them before you buy them. Otherwise, you'll probably just end up throwing them away.)
- Utensils which include: A ladle, a big spoon, a spatula, etc.
- A couple of large mixing bowls.
- A cast iron skillet. Note: You will have to season it by using the instructions that comes with it.
- A few good pots and pans. Spend a little more on these and they *will* last you a lifetime.

- A good set of steak knives.
- A good butcher knife.
- A knife sharpener.
- A handsome chef. (Don't you wish?)
- Cleaning supplies: Less is more: some spray cleaner with bleach, some liquid dishwashing detergent, Windex, etc. I put all of mine under the sink until I need them.
- Some dish towels, pot holders and oven mitts that you should gather up and wash once a week or so.
- A few trivets.
- Olive oil. (The best stuff to cook with.) Or your oil of choice.
- Paper towels and a paper towel holder, either wall-mounted or a counter.
- A microwave.
- Food. (Duh.)

Now let's get to it.

First clean the top of the cabinets:
- Get yourself a sturdy step ladder.
- Take all that stuff on top of the cabinets down. If you have any stuff on top of your cabinets, that is.
- If you have a lot of collectibles, consider finding another place for them and just put a few back. Or store/give away all of it.
- Wash these things in the sink and lay them on the counter on towels to dry. Or you can throw them in the dishwasher if they are, indeed, dishwasher safe.
- Take hand-vac and, using the step ladder, climb up and dust off the top of the cabinets. (Be safe!)
- If the top of the cabinets are greasy, get a cleaner with a degreasing agent in it and clean it thoroughly.

- Once you're done, replace only a few items back on top of the cabinets. Or don't put any of it back up there. (Saves having to do it again in the future.)

Now that you've got that under control, let's move on and tackle those cabinets.

Here's how to clean the inside of the cabinets:
- Open them up and one by one, empty every single one of them out.
- Now go through all of this stuff.
- Put it in piles of: Keep, throw away, charity or yard sale. (Obviously giving to charity or selling at a yard sale applies to old dishes, pot and pans, etc. and not food.)
- A word about pans: How many do you need? How many are rusted or look like they've been used as weapon to hit someone over the head? If it's deformed and rusted, get rid of it. You don't want to cook in that thing. (Bacteria can settle in cracks of pans.)
- As far as food items go, be sure to check the expiration dates on all of it and throw away if necessary.
- Take your hand-vac and vacuum all cabinets out. Vacuum the inside of the doors as well as the outside.
- Next, clean the cabinets. If they aren't wood, use a little bleach with water. If they are wood, use oil soap.
- Once the cabinets are dry, put all items you wish to keep back in them, neatly.
- You can buy a few stacking shelves to save space. Use them for smaller glasses and food items. You can even get a three-step shelf organizer for your canned goods and spices. This way, you get twice the amount of room in one cabinet.
- Close the doors and go over the outside of the cabinets with bleach water or oil soap or furniture polish—your call.

We all have drawers and drawers full of stuff we will never use. *If you have not used it within the last six months, throw it out or give it to charity.* Clear out every single one of those drawers and only put the things you are going to use back in.

The drawers:
- Open and empty them and one by one.
- Once drawers are empty, sort through stuff and make piles: Keep, throw away, charity or yard sale.
- Anything that needs to be washed, wash either in the sink or in the dishwater. (Cutlery, utensils, etc.)
- Next, vacuum inside each drawer, then clean with either bleach water or oil soap.
- Allow to dry.
- If you don't have a cutlery tray, go buy one. Make sure the one you buy has enough slots for your silverware. If you do have one, clean it as well and then put it back in the drawer with your freshly cleaned cutlery.

Everybody has a junk drawer. It's the drawer where you put stuff that doesn't really go anywhere else like batteries, fuses, whetstones, spare keys, etc. Also called the miscellaneous junk drawer. Let's get this thing organized in the simplest way possible.

A section devoted to the junk drawer tray:
- There is a tray you can buy that fits into a drawer and has about ten or so slots of all sizes and a sliding tray on top.
- It keeps everything organized and tidy.
- It will keep you from having to clean it out for a long, long time.
- You can find a junk drawer tray at about any store.
- Buy one and then put all of your miscellaneous stuff into it.

Phew! Glad that's done! Let's move it.

The refrigerator:
- You can take a day and do this by itself, if you like.
- You will need to empty the fridge and clean it from top to bottom.
- Take your hand-vac and suck up any stray crumbs or dust that's gathered.
- Using a little bleach water or your preferred cleaner, clean the inside of the fridge, from top to bottom. Take out the sliding drawers and shelves. Be sure to check if they're dishwasher safe and, if not, wash them in the sink.
- While shelves and drawers are drying, go through all of your food. Chuck any cheese that's moldy and any condiment that just has a little at the bottom. Be sure to check expiration dates on everything and chuck if it's out of date.
- Replace shelves and drawers.
- Put all food back into the fridge, close the door.
- Repeat process with freezer. If you don't have a defroster on your freezer, you will have to do it yourself by either turning off the fridge and letting it melt or by chipping away at the ice until you get it all off.
- Now remove all magnets and papers from outside of fridge.
- Take hand-vac and vacuum top of fridge off, then the outside of it.
- If you like, you can roll it out and vacuum the back of it off as well as the floor under it. (Be careful and get someone to help you if you have to!)
- Using bleach water or other cleaner, clean the entire surface of fridge.

- Now wipe off all magnets and then place them back on fridge.
- Done!

Time to clean the sink:
- You can do one of two things here.
- You can clean your sink with an abrasive cleaner like Comet. (Test first to see if it will scratch.) Just dust it in there and then wet it a little and let it sit for a few minutes. Then take a scrubber or a washcloth and scrub it out. Rinse by using the spray nozzle. There are non-abrasive cleaners that will work if abrasive cleaners aren't recommended.
- Or you can fill the sink with hot water and pour a little bleach in it. Let it sit for an hour or so, unplug it and it's done. (Use just a few ounces of bleach when you do this, nothing to overwhelm you as it is toxic stuff. If you like, open a window to let the fumes go.)

Are we ever going to be done? Soon, but not yet.

The kitchen counter:
- Take everything off of the counter.
- Take your hand-vac and vacuum every square inch of the counter.
- Depending on the surface, clean counter with the appropriate cleaner. I have a white counter, so I use a little bleach water that I spray on and let sit for a few minutes. This takes stains off very quickly.
- While the counter is soaking, go through everything you took off it and sort into piles: Keep, throw away, charity or yard sale.
- Whatever you have left, try to stow as much in the cabinets as possible, like the toaster and tea kettle. (You should have a lot more room now that you've cleaned them out.)

- Wipe counter off and use a few paper towels to dry it thoroughly.
- Wipe off all items going back on the counter.
- Some things that you need on counter: Butcher block set of knives, microwave, coffee maker. Nothing else really needs to go on the counter. If you still have a lot of stuff, try again to find a space in the cabinets for it.
- Freeing up counter space allows you to cook easier.

The most dreaded thing, the stove:

- If you have stove eyes, take them out, put them someplace safe and then take the drip pans and wash them. (They might need to soak. If so, run some water into sink, put in a little bleach and let them soak.)
- Take hand-vac and vacuum entire stove. Raise the top of the stove up by tugging at the front of it. Now vacuum in there.
- Now get a bottle of degreaser and spray it all over the stove. Let it soak for a few minutes.
- Wipe it off. (You may have to use quite a few paper towels to get it all done or a few old washcloths. If you have anything that's stuck on, get a small cleaning brush and try to get it off.)
- If you have any grime between the stove and counter, take a toothpick and run it along the edges.
- Now clean the oven of the stove with the *least* toxic stuff you can get. Just look in the store and find something that is "environmentally friendly" and follow the directions. Usually, you have to spray the cleaner on and then turn the stove on and let it sit. Then wipe away. (Always be sure to open a window and wear a mask if you can and wear your safety goggles.)
- If you have a self-cleaning over, hey, let it do its job.

- Next, pull out the stove drawer and empty it. Take your hand-vac and vacuum it out. If any of those pans or that grill pan is greasy, stick them in the dishwasher.
- Once you've got all the dust out from the drawer, spray some de-greaser in it and clean it out.
- Wipe and clean the hood of your stove.
- Now take the filter and light cover off, throw them in the sink and fill it with hot water. Pour a little bleach in and wait. These things get so nasty, it's unbelievable. You might have to let the filter sit for a while to dry. (Don't put it back up if it isn't dry!)
- The light cover should be ready in a few minutes.
- Replace drip pans and stove eyes and…
- Done!

If you can do that, you can do anything. So, last thing's last…

The floor:
- If you haven't washed your kitchen rugs in the washer, do it now.
- Now vacuum the entire floor.
- Now mop it. If you have linoleum, pour hot—but not *too* hot—water into a bucket then a little bleach. This will make those floors shine.
- If you have wood floors, use oil soap or whatever is recommended by the manufacturer.
- Allow to dry, replace rugs and you're done!

If you have a walk-in cupboard/pantry, just use the same guidelines when going through it and be sure to vacuum and mop the floor.

Here are a few quick tips:
- Always wipe your salt and pepper shaker off after you eat. They get so grimy, don't they?

- If you have a dish drainer, ask yourself if you need it. If you have to have one, buy one that's stylish and maybe even get one that's collapsible and can be stored away under the sink.
- Instead of a dish drainer, you can just lay a few dish towels out on the counter. When you wash dishes, put them on there and let them air dry. When they're dry, put them up and hang the dishtowel up to let it dry until you need it again. (You might have to wring it out a few times if you've had a big load of dishes.)
- If you have a dishwasher, one thing to do after your dishes are done is to let them air dry. Sometimes, the stuff doesn't get dry. I open the dishwasher up after it's done and then I turn the glasses upside down and let all the extra water drain off them. Never put dishes up that aren't fully dry because mold can form. *Ick!*

Brother! Look at how clean this place looks! It looks like a picture in a magazine, doesn't it? Yeah, and if you do a little here and there, it always will without much effort.

HERE'S HOW IT WORKS:
- Take a day and go over the entire kitchen.
- Start with the tops of the cabinets.
- Go to the inside of the cabinets.
- Clean out the drawers.
- Onto the refrigerator.
- Scrub the sink.
- Now tackle the counter.
- The stove is next.
- The floor is last.
- Done!

ANOTHER GIGANTIC TIME-SAVER—ALL WHITE TOWELS

Buy all white towels. Buy your bath towels and your hand towels and your dishtowels and even your oven mitts all in white. That way, you can throw them in the washer with your whites. Also, you can bleach these which means they'll be more sanitary.

MAGAZINES

I once had about five subscriptions to five different magazines. That meant I didn't have enough time to actually sit down and read them. Of course, this was money well wasted.

Keep a check on how many subscriptions you have. If you have over, say, five, it's time to let a few of them expire. No one has that much time to read magazines, do they? Not unless they work for one.

But you will still have a few here and there. Get something to put them in and stash it in an inconspicuous place in your living room. I keep mine next to a chair, next to the wall in a big basket. I also keep the phone book in there so I always know where it is.

Once you're done with your magazines, they can be donated to charity. Or you can recycle them. Or pawn them off on a friend or relative.

HERE'S HOW IT WORKS:
- Keep a check on magazine subscriptions.
- Get something to put all of them in, maybe even stow your phone book in there as well.

A FEW MORE ITTY-BITTY TIME-SAVERS

Itty-bitty time-saver:
- Buy a dry-erase board with magnets on the back and put it on your refrigerator.
- Whenever you need something for the house—or need to remember when a certain TV show comes on—write it down.
- When you make your list for the grocery store, all you have to do is copy from your board.
- This will save you so much time.

One more:
- Type all of you "important" numbers up and put it on the side of the refrigerator.
- For example: Dentist, bank, pizza place, movie theater—for show times—insurance agent, etc.
- Anyone that you need to call but don't want to keep on file—in your head, that is—can go on the list. This way, you don't have to find the phone book, call information or even track down an address book.

BOOKSHELVES

Bookshelves are a repository of all sorts of junk: CDs, knickknacks, maps, videos, DVDs, pictures, stereos and, of course, books. They inevitably seem to get overstuffed and overcrowded in no time. But it doesn't have to be this way.

It might be a good idea to take a whole day to go through every single bookshelf in your house and clean them. This is a tedious task that is best left to do by itself, instead of trying to incorporate it in while doing other tasks.

SUPPLIES YOU WILL NEED FOR THIS TASK:
- A hand-vac.
- Furniture cleaner.
- A few rags or paper towels.
- Windex.

While time consuming, it's pretty easy to do. Each shelf shouldn't take any longer than twenty or thirty minutes to do, tops.

Here's how you do it:
- Empty the entire bookshelf.
- Make three stacks: Keep, sell, charity.
- After that's done, vacuum your bookshelves from top to bottom.
- Maybe even pull the shelf out while it's empty and vacuum behind it. (Cobwebs love to hide back there.)
- If the shelves are wood, you might want to use a little furniture polish. Just spray all over and take a rag and wipe down. Be sure to let it dry thoroughly so the oil from the polish doesn't stain your books.

- If they're not made of wood but rather some sort of laminate, use some cleaner that's nonabrasive, like Windex and clean them. (Check an inconspicuous spot while doing this to be sure it doesn't discolor the board.)
- Vacuum off every book, CD, etc. with your hand-vac.
- And then stack everything neatly back into the shelves.
- Repeat process for all bookshelves.
- Phew. Thank God that's done.

Here's a tip: While alphabetizing may work in the library or bookstore, it probably won't work for you, especially if you buy a lot of books. You'll never be able to stop organizing them. The best way to organize your books is by category. That way you can add books easily and still stay organized. Also remember to leave yourself plenty of room to add books to your favorite categories.

If you have a lot of stuff to sell, you might want to consider going to a used bookstore. Many towns have used bookstores where you can sell or trade your old books, videos, DVDs and CDs. Are you still interested in backpacking in Siberia? Probably not. This is the kind of stuff that you want to get rid of.

Once you've got your pile of sell items, pack them in a few boxes and head out. Be warned, though, that when you take these items in, it can sometimes take up to an hour—or more—for them to go through your stuff. And, sometimes, they won't buy everything. So, most times, I just give all my old books to charity. The choice is yours.

However, you might want to consider keeping them for a yard sale. People love books at yard sales, though they will rarely pay over a dollar per book and, sometimes, they only want to pay twenty-five cents. Again, the choice is yours.

HERE'S HOW IT WORKS:

- Go through one bookshelf at a time.
- Empty it then sort into piles: Keep, charity, sell.
- Vacuum the entire shelf, even pull it out and vacuum behind it, then clean it with the cleaner of your choice.
- You can usually sell your old stuff to a used bookstore or you can keep it for a yard sale.

IN THE BATHROOM

Is your bathroom beginning to look like a beauty salon? How many half-empty bottles of shampoo do you have? You probably tell yourself that they're half-full, right? Regardless... How about hair spray? How about nail polish? Gather up the ones you know you will never use and give them to charity. (They will take items like this because many families come in for, well, charity and they need toiletries as well as other things.)

SUPPLIES YOU WILL NEED FOR THIS TASK:
- A hand-vac.
- Upright vacuum cleaner.
- A bottle of foam spray bathroom cleaner. (Scrubbing Bubbles type.)
- Windex.
- Paper towels.
- Toilet bowl cleaner.
- A toilet bowl brush.
- A few old washcloths.
- A mop.
- A bucket.

Before we begin, let's do a checklist of the basic things you need in your bathroom. Of course, this will vary from person to person.

All you need:
- A good moisturizer with SPF—sun protection factor for those of you who don't know. You can buy this at the super-store for about ten to fifteen bucks. Most of the

brands they carry are similar to the ones in department stores and they're lots cheaper. Check out the ingredients and you'll be surprised.

- One can of hairspray.
- If you do the mousse thing, one can of mousse.
- If you do the gel thing, one tube of gel.
- Frizz control stuff if you do the frizz control thing.
- Shampoo and conditioner.
- Tube of toothpaste/floss.
- Mouthwash. (Swish, swish.)
- Toothbrush and a couple of new ones to switch out about every three months. (Did you know your toothbrush collects germs? Throw them out often and get new ones.)
- Face wash.
- A can of shaving cream. (I wouldn't recommend using soap to shave your legs. Too many nicks and cuts.)
- Good razors. (If you buy the better ones, you can use them twice as long and they don't eat up your legs. I don't recommend buying ones with refills because you always forget what kind of refill to get and then you have to buy a whole new razor and start all over again. Just get the good disposables.)
- Toilet paper.
- Feminine products.
- Hand soap.
- Wash cloths.
- Toothbrush holder.
- Whatever make-up you use.
- Nice white fluffy towels.
- Your bathrobe.
- Your perfume.
- One bottle of good bubble bath or Mr. Bubbles if you prefer.
- A rubber duckie to keep you company.

- A bath mat. (You must have a bathmat. Spend a little extra and get one you can sink your toes into. Also, be sure it has a foam back so it doesn't skid across the floor.)
- A shower curtain.
- Any bathroom cleaning stuff which you will store under the sink.
- Hair dryer, curling iron if you use it. (Get one that turns itself off in case you forget so you won't have to worry about burning down the house.)
- A scale. (Spend a little extra and buy one that looks good and will last for years. About thirty to forty bucks will do it and it won't rust.)
- If applicable, the stuff the man in the house uses like aftershave lotion.
- If applicable, the stuff the kids use like baby shampoo.
- A cute, little trash can.

That's a lot of stuff!

If you have more stuff than this, then it's time to clear it out. What good is it doing you? Ask yourself when was the last time you used it and if it's not suntan lotion, it might be a good idea to chuck it. Also, stuff that doesn't belong in the bathroom, like tons of books and magazines, should be removed.

You might want to get a few cleaning supplies to keep under the sink as well. That way, you don't have to carry the stuff around and, when the mood hits you to clean, you'll have it all at your disposal. You don't need much in there. You can buy smaller bottles of the stuff so it doesn't take up so much room. I don't use those cleaning cloths because I've found they never get things as clean as I like. (Good rule of thumb: When cleaning, never, *ever* throw paper towels—or those cleaning cloths—down the toilet because they will clog it up!)

Cleaning supplies I have:

- A bottle of foam spray bathroom cleaner which is used for the sink and the bathtub. (Scrubbing Bubbles type.)
- A small bottle of Windex.
- Paper towels.
- A bottle of toilet bowl cleaner.
- A toilet bowl brush which is in its own little container and stuck in the corner behind the commode.
- A few old washcloths.

That's all you need. Ready to clean? But before you start, grab your bathmat and take down your shower curtain and put them into the washing machine. Separately, of course. And use a couple of dryer sheets so they'll smell nice and fresh.

A note on the shower curtain: I buy cloth shower curtains because not only do they look better, but they last longer and are more stylish. Also, you can throw them into the wash. You can get a good one for about twenty bucks. Kmart seems to have the best selection.

Before you do any of this, go to the store and pick up a few of those little stacking shelves that are designed for kitchen cabinets. I have two of the larger sizes. (Be sure to measure before you go!) Slip those shelves in your vanity and you will have room to stack your stuff. Stuff can go on top and stuff can go on bottom. But first thing's first.

It's time to tackle the medicine cabinet:

- Open it up and empty it of its contents.
- Separate into piles: Keep, throw away and charity, if applicable.
- Shake all of the cans of hairspray, etc. and see how uch is in there. If not a lot, chuck it.
  - ab your hand-vac and vacuum it out. Yeah, dust les there, too, and it's a lot easier to vacuum dust

than to wipe it off. Also, vacuum the entire outside of the cabinet and the top. (Use a sturdy step ladder or chair to get up there.)

- Now take an old washcloth and some spray cleaner—some with bleach—and wipe down. If your cabinet is wood, use oil soap—and clean it from top to bottom.
- Place the stuff you're going to keep in sections. Hair products on one shelf, toothpaste and mouthwash on another and so on and so forth until it is completely and utterly organized.
- Close the door and Windex the mirror.
- Buy a stylish little bowl to put all your tiny items like tweezers, nail files, clippers, etc. in and put it on top of the medicine cabinet or, if it will fit, inside the medicine cabinet. Next time you're looking for your tweezers, there they will be. (Sometimes you can find really neat little bowls at antique stores for a couple bucks each.)

It already feels so much better in there, doesn't it?

Inside of the vanity:
- Sit down on the floor and open the door on the vanity.
- Pull *every single thing* out of there—tampons and toilet paper and the like.
- As you remove everything, put stuff in piles: Keep, throw away and charity. Maybe you've got four or five curling irons. You only need one. Pick the best one and send the rest packing.
- Once that's done, vacuum it out.
- Then clean it with the cleaner of your choice from top to bottom.
- Now vacuum the outside of the vanity, from top to bottom.

- Use the cleaner and clean it all over, even getting into little crevices.
- Replace all the items you're keeping. If you got some stacking shelves, put them in first, then stack the other stuff in.
- Shut the door and breathe a sigh of relief.

If you have drawers on the vanity, just use the same method to clean them out as you did the kitchen drawers.

The top of the sink/vanity:
- Clear everything off, putting it somewhere so it's not in your way.
- Depending on the surface of the vanity, it's best to use a cleaner that's appropriate. If you can use something like Comet to clean it, then do so. Otherwise, use some spray bathroom cleaner.
- Spray the cleaner on and then use an old washcloth to scrub it clean. (Use a little extra elbow grease so it'll sparkle.)
- Next, using Windex, spray the faucet till it's shiny.
- Now replace all that stuff you had on there to begin with.

If you have a linen closet:
- Open the door.
- Pull everything out.
- Sit down and go through it and separate into piles: Keep, throw away and charity. (Any old towels that aren't threadbare can go to charity, otherwise, just chuck them.)
- Take your hand-vac and dust from top to bottom, including the shelves and the door.
- Fold towels neatly and put everything back into categories: Toilet paper on one shelf, towels on another, etc.

Moving on to…

The bathtub:
- Remove all of your shampoos and soaps and lotions and all that out of the bathtub and place on the floor.
- Sit down and go through it and get rid of anything you haven't used in the last month or two.
- Take your hand-vac and vacuum off the top of the tub, then take a washcloth and run it along the top of the tub, too. (All kinds of dust settles there.)
- Next, if you have a tile bathtub, you will need to get something like Tilex to get the mold out. Otherwise, you can just a foaming cleaner like Scrubbing Bubbles.
- If you have shower door, you will need to spray it down, too.
- Spray the entire tub and let it soak for about twenty minutes.
- After your cleaner has set a few minutes, grab your washcloth, turn on the faucet and wet it. Go from top to bottom until you have cleaned the entire tub. Pay special attention to the faucet and the shower head and clean those as well. As you do this, keep rinsing your washcloth out.
- Depending on how dirty your bathtub is, you might have to get a scrub brush to get some of the grime off.
- After this, rinse the entire tub out using your shower head. Or you can get a bucket, fill it with water and rinse that way.
- After you've gone through all of your shampoos and lotions and potions, put only the things you know you are going to use back into the tub.
- If you don't have a shower caddy—one that hangs on the shower head—buy one of those to put your toiletries on. They save lots of space. Be sure to buy one

in white plastic and not stainless steel because the steel ones are hard to clean and rust in about a month.

The toilet:

- Using your hand-vac, vacuum the entire outside of the toilet off.
- Put some toilet bowl cleaner in the toilet and let it soak.
- Get a washcloth and wet it with hot water and wipe the toilet down from top to bottom.
- Scrub out the bowl with a toilet bowl brush.
- Done!

And lastly...

The floor:

- Vacuum the floor.
- Then mop it using a little water and bleach.
- Let it dry then replace your clean bathmat.
- After that's finished, put your shower curtain up.

And that's it. Phew! Time to watch some TV.

HERE'S HOW IT WORKS:

- Start on the bathroom by cleaning out the medicine cabinet.
- From there, go to the vanity and clean it out.
- Then clean the vanity top.
- Now go on to the linen closet.
- Move to the bathtub.
- Now everyone's favorite, the toilet bowl.
- Vacuum and mop the floor.
- Put up the shower curtain, then throw the bathmat on the floor.
- Done!

WHY DIDN'T I THINK OF THAT? OVER-THE-DOOR TOWEL RACKS

If you're short on space in the bathroom or you don't like hanging towel racks everywhere, why not buy one of those over-the-door towel racks? They're easy to install and most times all you have to do is hang them, put in one little screw and you're done. The white plastic ones never rust and you have a ton of little hooks for all your towels and your bathrobe. And it doesn't take up precious wall space.

Just a thought.

HERE'S HOW IT WORKS:
- Buy an over-the-door towel rack and save wall space.
- Have plenty of room for your towels and your bathrobe.

IN THE BEDROOM

This is the easiest room in the house for me to clean. I actually don't mind doing it. Let's get to it.

SUPPLIES YOU WILL NEED FOR THIS TASK:
- A hand-vac.
- Upright vacuum cleaner.
- A mop—if you don't have carpet.
- A bucket—ditto.
- Windex.
- Paper towels.

Ready? Set. Go!

Cleaning the bedroom:
- Strip the bed and take all of your bed linens to the washer, even your comforter, even the dust ruffle. (Note: If you have a huge comforter, you might have to go to the Laundromat to wash it as it might not fit into your washer.)
- Grab your upright vacuum cleaner and—I know this sounds crazy—climb up on the bed and vacuum the mattress. If you'd rather use your hand-vac, you can do that. But you do need to vacuum the mattress at least twice a year. It gets rid of dust mites and the like. It makes everything smell nicer, too.
- If you have a water bed, you obviously don't have to worry about this.
- You've already tackled the closet, so you can ignore it for the time being.

- Now get your hand-vac and dust all surfaces. You will have to pick everything up off the dresser surface to do this. Remember to vacuum your knickknacks as you go.
- A few times a year, it might be a good idea to go over your furniture with some furniture polish.
- After you're done with all the dusting/vacuuming, Windex the mirror—or mirrors. When did you get that one on your ceiling?! Anyway, that's between you and…you.
- Now, it's time to move the furniture out so you can vacuum under it. Get someone to help you do this! You will throw your back out if you don't!
- If you don't have someone handy, just use your hand-vac around the corners. If you can move little items like the nightstand, vacuum under it and then replace. But never—never—do this on your own and hurt yourself. A clean house isn't worth a trip to the emergency room!
- Time to vacuum the carpet.
- If you don't have carpet, vacuum the floor and then mop it.
- After you're done with that, get your freshly laundered bedclothes and make up the bed.

Take a look around and see if you've missed anything. You've cleaned this room from top to bottom and it looks great, doesn't it? Lie on the bed and take a nap. You've earned it.

Note: If you have more than one bedroom, all you have to do is repeat this process until all of the rooms are cleaned.

HERE'S HOW IT WORKS:

- Launder all bedclothes.
- Vacuum mattress.
- Dust all surfaces with hand-vac.
- Move furniture as you can to vacuum under.
- Windex mirrors.
- Vacuum carpet and/or floors, then mop.
- Make up bed.
- Take a nap.

CARPET CLEANING

It is a wise investment to buy a stream cleaner to clean your carpets. If you can afford to buy one, they run about two-hundred bucks and you can buy them at any Wal-Mart. Be sure to get one that's looks like an upright vacuum and has a long cord. Also, you will have to buy the carpet cleaner to go in the machine. This usually runs about ten to twenty bucks a bottle.

If you're lucky, you can borrow one from a friend or a relative and save yourself the money.

Either way, it's a good idea to clean the carpets about once a year. If you have kids, once a year probably won't cut it. More than likely, you'll have to do it three or four times a year or whenever they get dirty.

Also, it's a good idea to clean carpets in warmer weather because they will dry more quickly.

HERE'S HOW TO DO IT:

- Before you steam clean the carpets, you will need to vacuum them thoroughly.
- Pay attention to corners of your room as dust collects there. Take an attachment and vacuum if necessary.
- If at all possible, remove all furniture from rooms when you steam clean carpets. If not possible, just go around the furniture as best you can.
- Using the instructions on the steam cleaner, get it ready and then clean the carpets. You might have to empty out the container a few times, depending on the size of your room. (The water gets really dirty, too, so empty it into the bathtub.)

- This will take about thirty minutes per room.
- Once you're finished, be sure to let the carpet dry. Don't go tracking in there to look for something.
- It might take half a day or so to *completely* dry, so if you have to go in the room, wear clean socks.
- Once your carpet is *completely* dry, put all furniture back if you've removed it.
- You now have a nice, clean carpet to enjoy.

CODE RED!

Did you know that if you don't have a fire extinguisher in your home and it burns, the insurance may not pay for anything? It's true. Go today and buy one. You can get a little, house-sized one for less than twenty bucks.

Be sure to read the instructions and maybe even practice a few times so you'll know how to use it. This universally known system is called "PASS" and goes a little something like this…

PASS:
- Pull pin.
- Aim at *base* of fire, press trigger. (Remember to always aim at the base of the fire and not the flames as this is where the fire builds and grows!)
- Squeeze trigger.
- Sweep/spray from side to side.

It's very important that you understand how to use this thing. Make time to study the instructions.

Another good thing to have around is a fire-proof safe or box. You can get these for fifty bucks or less and they store all the things you need like passports and birth certificates and old pictures you cherish. If you keep extra money lying around the house, you can put that in there as well.

A few more safety tips:
- Have a safety plan if a fire breaks out. If you live in a two-story dwelling, buy a safety ladder that you can hang off an upstairs window. (You can buy this at any home improvement store.)

- Check your smoke detector and never disable it for anything—even if you've just burned the toast! Be sure to replace the batteries as needed.
- If you live in a two-story home, be sure to have a smoke detector on the top floor as well.
- Make sure you have a land-line phone and not just a cordless. You can keep this in the closet if you like, but keep one handy. When the power goes out, your cordless won't work.
- It wouldn't hurt to also get a carbon monoxide detector as well.
- Make copies of all papers. Keep in your fire-proof box.
- If you can, scan favorite old photographs into your computer and maybe even put them on a disc to keep in your fire-proof box.

It is also a good idea to call your insurance agent from time to time to make sure all your valuables are covered. If you rent, and can afford it, get some renters' insurance.

HERE'S HOW IT WORKS:
- Buy yourself a house-sized fire extinguisher.
- Get a fire-proof safe or box for important papers.
- Never disable a smoke detector for anything.
- Have a safety plan in case fire breaks out.
- Consider investing in a carbon monoxide detector.
- Make copies of all important papers.
- Get a fire/safety ladder for your upstairs.
- Get a land-line phone in case the power goes out.

AIR CONDITIONER FILTERS

If you have an air-conditioning unit or heat pump that has a filter, replace or clean the filter at least once a month. It saves money on your electric bill and also keeps the dust filtered out of your air. It wouldn't be a bad idea to use your hand-vac on vents every few months, either.

You can also buy filters that last up to three months. They're a little more expensive but worth it, in my opinion.

HERE'S HOW IT WORKS:
- Clean air-conditioning/heat pump filter at least once a month.
- This keeps your air cleaner and saves on the electric bill.
- Be sure to vacuum all the vents in your house every few months. Even the ones in the ceiling.
- You can buy some filters that last up to three months. A wise investment if I ever heard of one.

CURTAINS

Curtains can look really good and add some piazza to a room. However, they do get dusty over time and need to be cleaned occasionally. A good going over with a vacuum cleaner attachment—with brush—or a hand vac is never a bad idea. However, about once a year, it might be a good idea to take them down and wash them. And, while you're at it, wash the window the curtain is covering. (We'll discuss this in depth in the next chapter.)

The best way to tackle this job is to take one room at a time and take the curtains down and wash them. Of course, some curtains must go to the dry cleaner, so be sure to check the manufacture's instructions, usually on the tag. If your curtains can go into the wash, throw them in there and then go back to the dreaded window washing.

HERE'S HOW YOU DO IT:
- Go around to every window in your house and remove your curtains.
- Check to make sure all of them can go into the washer.
- If so, put them into washer, if not, take them to the dry cleaners.
- Once they're done, throw them into the dryer for about ten minutes or so with a dryer sheet. (Keep an eye on this as you don't want them to shrink! Always read the care instruction tag.)
- Now wash the windows.
- Then hang them back up while they're still a little damp.
- The wrinkles—depending on the fabric—should fall right out without ironing.

WASHING WINDOWS—AND WALLS

Windows do not have to be that big of a pain in the butt. I know, I know that they are. But once you get them clean, you won't have to worry about them for a year or so.

Same goes for walls. Just take a day to do everything and you can relax for a long time.

SUPPLIES YOU WILL NEED FOR THIS TASK:
- A hand-vac.
- Windex.
- Paper towels.
- A Webster or a broom.

Here's how to clean windows with as little pain as possible:
- Remove curtains and/or pull up blinds.
- Get your hand-vac and vacuum the window.
- Clean the window with Windex. (For some reason, it's better to clean windows on cloudy days—less streaking.)
- Pull the shade down and vacuum it while you're at it. (You can also go ahead and wash curtains while you clean the windows and it's all done at once.)

A note: if you have windows that are too high to reach, you can get window cleaners that you attach to the garden hose. Do this to clean the outside. If you can't reach the window without risking injury, it might be a good idea to call in a professional. Just a thought. However, never risk climbing up high to clean a window. It's not worth it. Just do the best you can with the garden hose or just call a professional, budget permitting, of course.

Now let's talk about cleaning the walls and the ceiling. I only occasionally do this. You can do it as often as you like, or whenever you see a stray cobweb. I have this thing called the Webster. It's a stick with a bunch of furry looking plastic things sticking out of the top of it. Its purpose is to get the ceiling and walls free of cobwebs. It works and I advise you to get one.

For the walls:
- You can use a vacuum attachment on your upright to go up and down walls occasionally to suck the dust off.
- While you're doing this, vacuum the baseboards and door frames as well.
- About once a year, go over baseboards and door frames with a little lemon oil if they're wood. If they're painted, use an appropriate cleaner or just a damp washcloth.

For the ceiling:
- Use something like a Webster or a broom with a dust rag on it. If you have dark paint, you'll want to avoid scratching your ceiling.
- If you want to climb onto a sturdy chair or step-ladder, you can take your hand-vac and suck away the dust up there.

Wall mirrors and pictures:
- Now go after all the pretty pictures on your walls.
- Vacuum all of them off and Windex if necessary.
- Done!

That wasn't so bad, was it?

HERE'S HOW IT WORKS:

- Take a day to get this big task done.
- Start by removing and washing curtains.
- Now pull up blinds and vacuum the entire window.
- After that, Windex the windows.
- Get a Webster or a broom and go after all the cobwebs on you walls and ceiling.
- Put curtains back up.
- Next, clean all of the stuff on your walls like pictures and windows.
- Done for about a year or so.

AN ITTY-BITTY MONEY-SAVER—WASHING CLOTHES IN COLD WATER

I always, always wash all of my clothes on cold in the washer. I do not see the need in washing *anything* in hot water. The water, it seems to me, doesn't get hot enough to really sanitize anything. Also, I use bleach on whites and color safe bleach on colors, so what's the point of using hot water? Nada. Also, the dryer gets the clothes pretty hot, so doesn't that sanitize them? I believe so.

By doing this, it really saves on my electric bill. If you want to see if it'll save you any money on your electric bill, why not give it a try?

HERE'S HOW IT WORKS:
- I wash all of my clothes on cold in the washer.
- I don't see any reason to wash anything on hot.
- Try it and see.

THE REMOTE CONTROLS

I know some people who have some really nasty and sticky and dirty remote controls. I won't pick them up when I visit because it's just so…*ick.*

Take a minute to assess your remote control situation. If they're dirty, grab all the remotes and wipe them off. You can use an old washcloth and some Windex. Be warned, however, that Windex might take a little of the color off. But at least they'll be clean.

However, don't clean the remotes with water and certainly don't get any funny ideas about submersing them in water.

Also, you can take a toothpick and clean the crevices of the remote. Just slide it in there and have a paper towel handy to wipe the grime onto.

If you're a person who's always losing their remote controls, a good way to organize them is to buy a funky looking bowl or a basket and put it on your coffee table. Now throw all the remotes into it. And then you'll never lose them again. After we turn off the TV, we chuck the remote into the bowl. Easy to find and when I clean, I just pick them up as I'm dusting and let my hand-vac suck all the dust away.

Don't neglect your remote controls.

HERE'S HOW IT WORKS:
- Clean remotes with an old washcloth and some Windex and toothpicks to get the grime out of crevices.
- Buy a bowl or a basket and put it on the coffee table.
- Throw all remotes into the basket/bowl.
- When dusting, dust the remotes.
- No more looking for the control.

IN THE LIVING ROOM

Let's just assume, for argument's sake, that we all just have one living room and that's where the TV is located. I know lots of people have great rooms and dens and family rooms. That's cool if you do, and, if you do, just use these same guidelines to clean those additional rooms.

SUPPLIES YOU WILL NEED FOR THIS TASK:
- A hand-vac.
- Upright vacuum cleaner.
- Furniture polish.
- A mop.
- A bucket.
- Windex.
- Paper towels.
- A few rags.

One way to take less work out of cleaning the living room is to take out some of the furniture.

Assess your situation:
- Take a look around the living room and see if there is anything you can get rid of. An extra chair here or there, an extra plant stand?
- Do you have too many pictures on the wall? Too many knickknacks? If so, why not get rid of a few?
- How about that stack of magazines? Go through them and get rid of as many as possible. If you have newspapers or any other kind of papers lying around, chuck those as well. (You should have already gathered

this junk up but if you don't, please do yourself a favor and do it now.)
- Remember, if you don't use it, chuck it.
- If you find you want to get rid of a few things, put them somewhere to save for your yard sale or take them to charity.

Now that that's done, let's get to cleaning:
- Start by using your hand-vac to dust/vacuum everything.
- Every surface, every knickknack, everything needs to be dusted.
- Once that's done, why not get a little furniture polish and make all the wood in your living room shine? Go for it.
- After that, move the couch and chairs and vacuum under them as well as the tables. (I can't move my TV stand, so I just dust around it, taking the long vacuum hose attachment and sliding it between the wall and stand.)
- Now head over to the TV and once you've vacuumed it off, take some Windex and clean it—be sure to use caution and read manufacture's instructions before cleaning LCD or plasma screens. Depending on how long it's been neglected, it might take several paper towels to get it clean. Be sure to turn the TV OFF before you start cleaning!
- Vacuum the floor and then, if necessary mop it. Remember, oil soap for wood and a little bleach with water for tile or linoleum. If it's laminate, just a little warm water and a mop will do the trick. If you have carpet, just vacuum.
- And you're done! Ta da!

IN THE LIVING ROOM

The living room is probably the easiest place for me to keep clean. Once you've done the good once-over, it should be for you to keep clean, too.

Now just take these same principals and apply them to the dining room, mud room or any other additional rooms.

HERE'S HOW IT WORKS:
- See if there's any extra piece of furniture you can get rid of and, if so, get rid of it.
- Start by using your hand-vac to dust every surface off.
- Use a little furniture polish on your wood.
- Move the couch and tables and vacuum under them.
- Clean the TV with Windex. Make sure it's turned off!
- Vacuum/mop floor.
- Done!

STAIRWAY TO HEAVEN

If you have stairs in your house, take a little time to get them clean. It's not that hard.

How to clean the stairs:
- Take your hand-vac and vacuum them from top to bottom, whether you have carpet or wood.
- If you have wood stairs, mop them off with oil soap. Or you can get a bucket of warm water, add a little oil soap and get an old rag. Dip the rag in and then wring, then clean the stairs with the rag, dipping and wringing as necessary. This might be an easier way to do it as you can also clean the spindles as you go. (Be sure to let the stairs completely dry before anyone uses them.)
- Vacuum the spindles.
- If you have wood spindles, use a little lemon oil to make them shine. Just get an old rag, put a little lemon oil on and then shine them right up!
- Painted spindles can be cleaned with a non-abrasive cleaner like Fantastic. (Always test first to make sure it doesn't take the paint off.) Or you can just use water and a rag.

DON'T FORCE YOURSELF TO LIVE IN A MUSEUM

I think most of us have too much junk.

Junk complicates our lives but we can't seem to part with this or with that for whatever reason. I don't abide by that anymore. At one time, my house was filled with so much junk I was about to go crazy. I got tired of always moving stuff around and bumping into it. One day, I'd had enough. Now if there's something in my house and I don't need it, I either sell it or give it away.

Less is more. Just think about it. It's true. If you have less junk, you have less to worry about and keep up with. Once you've got the main pieces of furniture—couch, bed, etc.— anything extra is nothing but extra work. If you've inherited some piece of furniture and just absolutely hate it but can't sell or donate it, why not ask a member of your family if they would like it? I'm sure it wouldn't upset anyone. If anyone asks, just tell them you didn't have room for it anymore.

We all get saddled with something no one else wants. I have a friend who just bought a new home. His parents basically cleaned out their garage and gave him all the old junk out of it. Now he has all this junk like an old chest with scratches all over it and rickety old dining table. And the kicker is, he can't get rid of it or "It'll make mom mad."

This happens to the best of us. I inherited some dishes from my grandmother. They sat in my cabinet for years, untouched. They also took up a bunch of space I could have used. I finally asked my mother if she would take them off my hands and she did. This cleared up a bunch of cabinet space for me. I also inherited my grandmother's old bedroom suit and though I loved it, I had no where to put it. I moved it from one room and then to another other room and then to the closet. For about five years, I moved that thing so many times, I was about to chop it up for firewood.

I told my mom I couldn't handle it anymore. I had to get rid of it and she said, "I know someone who can use it. Do you want to see if they want it?"

Absolutely. If someone else can use it and benefit from it, who am I to tell them no? I gave it away to a family member who needed it more than I did. It makes me feel good to have done something nice for someone else.

I have my special memories of my grandmother and I just don't think I have to keep an old bedroom suit around to remind me of her. I have a picture of us together when I was a baby that I keep in my bedroom. I look at it just about every day and remember her that way, holding me in her arms. Now I don't have to stump my toe or throw my hands up in frustration while trying to find room for her bedroom suit. Now someone else can get some use out of it instead of it sitting in a closet going to pot.

If you have anything you have to take "special" care with, what is the use in having it? If you have a Louis XIV chair that no one can sit in it, what's the point? Of course, not many of us have these kinds of chairs, but if you have something that's so "special" you have to treat it "specially," you're just giving yourself extra work. And you have to worry about someone "messing it up." You might want to keep some special things, but you have to have the room for it.

My motto is: Use it or give it away. Of course, if you have something of value, you'll want to sell it and not give it away.

Everything single room in my house has a function and most everything in it has a use. I don't care for a lot of knickknacks—i.e. a lot of extra dusting—and I don't care to have a chair I can't let anyone sit in. I do have a few things I don't need, like an old clock or two. But those are for decoration and when I see these things, I smile because I like them. I just don't go overboard and neither should you. And neither should anyone make you by pawning off old junk they no longer want but can't justify selling or giving away to charity.

I know someone who has a gazillion house plants. She doesn't need that many and they're everywhere, on everything. It looks like a greenhouse in there. She has to take time every day to water and sometimes "feed" them and then she has to move them around to clean and dust. And she wonders why she doesn't have any extra time.

Don't force yourself to live in a museum. Make your house comfortable and make it livable. That way, you have less work to do and you can enjoy your home more. You're paying for it, after all. Use it for what it is: A place you can call home.

HERE'S HOW IT WORKS:

- If someone pawns something off on you that you don't want, give it away or ask them to take it back.
- If you don't have any room in your house for the things you like and instead have all this stuff you have to "cherish," what's the point?
- Don't force yourself to live in a museum.

CEILING FIXTURES

All of us neglect our overhead light fixtures. I know I do and, boy, do they get grimy.

Why not take a day and go through the entire house cleaning them? Once you have all of them up to snuff, you can just clean them occasionally or when you change the light bulb.

It's easy:

- Get a sturdy step-ladder or chair.
- Climb up and, using your hand-vac, vacuum the fixture off.
- If it's a little greasy or grimy, use some Windex to clean it.
- If you have ceiling fans, the best way to clean them is, again, with your hand-vac. After you've got all the accumulated dust off, grab some Windex and wipe it clean. Or just use a slightly damp old rag and wipe off.
- Phew, aren't you glad that's done?

A CHEAP WAY TO GET RID OF ANTS

Around the spring of the year, I usually get some new critters and not the cute/cuddly kind. Ants. Little black ants just march right in. And, no, I didn't invite them.

Since I can't ask them to leave, I do something else. And this something helps not only my pocketbook but it helps the environment as well.

If you find that you have ants—and don't want them—go buy a few apples. Yeah, you heard me. Go get a few apples and cut them up and then place them where the ants are. The ants will take the apple to their queen and because she can't digest the apple, she will eat it and die and then her colony will die. Yup, her followers can't survive without her. And that means the ants will go away.

You can even do this outside if you like. It works anywhere.

The building I used to work in was once infested with these huge ants. I went to the store and got some apples and in a few days, they all disappeared. Gone! Goodbye! Everyone thought I'd lost my mind or something when I set the apples out, but once it worked, they looked at me with admiration and awe.

It works. It's weird that it works, but it does, indeed work.

Another thing about bugs. Bugs, cockroaches especially, like cardboard boxes. In actuality, they *love* cardboard boxes. If you have any of these just sitting around, why not replace them with plastic ones? Might save a trip from the exterminator.

HERE'S HOW IT WORKS:
- Apples+Ants=Gone.
- Bugs love cardboard boxes. Replace with plastic.

YARD SALE!

Those are my mother's two favorite words. If we're going somewhere together and she sees a yard sale sign, she nearly passes out with excitement. "We can find some good stuff! Let's go! *Now!*"

While yard sale might be her two favorite words, when she hears the words, "Four-family yard sale!" she gets a glazed look in her eye. It's unnerving. It's like she's reaching nirvana or something.

You might not have this same reaction. In fact, you might not have even *thought* about yard sales one way or the other. However, if you've been de-cluttering, you've probably got a bunch of stuff that you might not want to give away but still want to get rid of. The best way to get rid of it? Have a yard sale.

Think about it before you commit, though. Do you want to sell your junk at a yard sale? If you have a lot, it might be worthwhile. I've known people who've made tons of money and they got rid of all their old junk to boot. However, yard sales can be annoying. It's important to keep in mind, these things can and will drive you crazy. You have to put a price on everything, set a date, pick a place, put out signs, etc.

On the other side of this, know that valuable pieces of furniture or oil paintings should be sold on Ebay or through an auction house. You might have to end up giving them away at a yard sale. You can sometimes find used furniture and/or antique stores to consign in. Keep in mind, though, that you will have to take the stuff there. Be sure to borrow a truck.

So, if you want to have a yard sale, I say go for it. That is, if you have a yard. If you live in a big neighborhood, see if it has an annual yard sale and maybe go in with some of your neighbors. If you live in an apartment complex, contact the manager and see if you can get one started there. Sometimes churches have yard sales, too. Just check around.

And if you can't swing a yard sale, take your junk to charity and get it out of your site.

The bright side of having your own yard sale is that you only have to do it once to get rid of all that stuff. And once it's gone and you have that money in your hand, you can take yourself and someone you love to a really nice dinner. Or you could save it. (I'd go to dinner, personally.)

I've said this once, but I'll say it again. Clothes don't usually sell well at yard sales unless you want to sell them all for a quarter. Ditto with your old CDs and videos. Like I said before, if you want to get rid of them, there is always a used bookstore in every town that is willing to take this stuff off your hands. It's just a little better than giving it away, but not much. However, if you don't watch/listen to it anymore, you can either sell it or use it for a coaster.

But if you still want to have a yard sale, here's how to do it right. Keep in mind that if you've never been to a yard sale before, it might be a good idea to go to a few to get the gist of it.

THE BASICS OF YARD SALES:

- Sort everything out in piles according to what it is: CDs, clothing, cookware, etc.
- Get some labels and cut them in half and put a label on every single thing.
- Get a magic marker and put a price on every label which is now stuck to every single thing.
- Consider how much you want for something. Clothes, between a fifty-cents and a dollar if you're not

consigning them. Leather coats in good shape, fifteen to twenty dollars. Cookware, depending on shape, between two and three, CDs a few dollars, books a quarter or fifty cents and so on and so forth. Larger items, like furniture in good shape, should go for at least twenty-five bucks but if you haven't sold it by afternoon, start asking people if they want it for free to haul it off for you.

- Pick your date and time.
- Buy some poster boards to make signs and little stakes to put them in the ground with. Make sure the signs have your address on them and an arrow pointing in the right direction! Also put the date on there.
- Consider putting your yard sale in the newspaper.
- On the day of your yard sale, get up early and distribute signs all over the place. The more the better.
- Go back home and start hauling the stuff out into the yard. If you have a table or two you can put it on, even better.
- Get a lawn chair and wait for the crowd. They will come, believe me. However, don't get discouraged if they don't come for an hour or so. Other people are probably having yard sales, too.
- When someone tries to bargain with you, bargain with them. You don't want this stuff back in your house, believe me. Get rid of it.
- When afternoon comes, start telling people they can have everything cheaper. Maybe do a "buy one, get one free" thing.
- Be friendly with your "customers" and even suggest things for them to buy.
- When it's all said and done, pack everything up that's left and take it to a charity drop-off center. If you have furniture, call a few used furniture shops and ask if they'd like it. (Might be a good idea to do this

beforehand so you won't have to deal with it. They will usually give you about as good a price as a yard sale customer.)

- Count your money. Whoohoo!
- Take a long shower and go out to dinner. You deserve it.

ANOTHER ITTY-BITTY MONEY-SAVER—BUY GENERIC

I always buy generic washing detergent. I have found it does do the job about as good as the name brands. (And I always buy liquid detergent because it seems that the powdered kind always clumps up and stays on clothes. If you dry this stuff on your clothes, you've got to throw it back in the washer again to get it off.)

Also, most cleaning supplies are the same. However, the generic brands sometimes cost a dollar or so less than the name brands. Think about buying these products in generic and then see how much money you save.

HERE'S HOW IT WORKS:
- Generic cleaning supplies usually have the exact some ingredients as brand name ones.
- Consider switching and see how much money you save.

THINGS EVERY HOME SHOULD HAVE

We all have lots of junk in our homes. Some of it we need and some of it, we don't. And sometimes, we *don't* have things we need. This means, we're always going out to the store to get this stuff. It usually happens when we're trying to hang a picture or putting together a shelf.

Why not go over what you have and then see what you need? Take a day to do this and buy all those little things that will make your life easier.

And here's a list that might help you as well…

A toolbox and or plastic shoe boxes which include:

- An electric screwdriver with two heads: Flat *and* Phillips head.
- A hammer.
- A box of nails.
- Some duct tape to help with those pesky husbands and/or boyfriends! (Just kidding!)
- A flashlight.
- Batteries in all sizes.
- A measuring tape.
- Needle nose pliers.
- A small crescent wrench.
- A pair of wire pliers.
- A razor knife.
- Plastic anchors for hanging stuff.

Other things every home should have:

- A fire extinguisher.

- A fireproof box to put all your important papers in: Birth certificate, passport, etc.
- An alarm clock with battery back-up.
- Good all cotton sheets. With all the money you're going to save—or make!—you can get the higher thread count, which is so luxurious it should be a sin.

What else do you need if you have all this? Not much.

THIRTY MINUTES OR LESS TO A CLEAN HOUSE

Now that you have your entire house sparkling clean, it's time to do the thirty minutes or less routine to a clean house. This should not be difficult if you've already got everything cleaned and out of the way. All you will have to do from now on is maintain it. This shouldn't be hard if you've already done the big stuff like de-cluttering and de-griming.

Once you get everything clean, you can do this in increments of five or ten minutes here or there. You don't have to do it all at once. Just pick up something off the floor when you see it instead of ignoring it and make it a habit to always clean the kitchen counter after you've eaten. Doing little stuff like that here and there will save you a lot of headaches later on.

And you don't have to dust your entire house every week, either. I usually just dust the living room and then sometimes, just run a cloth over the tables.

The point is to take action when you start to see things going a little awry. If you take care of the problem right then, you don't have to do another deep clean for a year or so. But if you wait until everything has gone to pot, you're going to have to start all over again.

This is not hard and it won't take any time to explain it. How to do it in thirty minutes or less:

The bathroom:
- Once a week, clean the bathrooms by putting some cleaner into the toilet bowl and spot cleaning the vanity/sink top.
- Windex the medicine cabinet.

- Check the medicine cabinet ever so after to make sure stuff isn't piling up.
- Grab the vacuum and run it over the floor and bathmat.

The living room:
- Now, take your hand-vac and dust everything in the living room off.
- Pick up any stray items—magazines, remote controls, etc—and put them in their proper place, whether in my magazine basket or in the trash.
- Vacuum the floor.
- If floor needs to be mopped, get a bucket of water and mop it using the appropriate cleaner—oil soap for wood, beach for tile, Mop&Glo, etc.
- Be sure to vacuum/dust TV and other electronics.
- Living room is done and took about ten minutes.

The kitchen:
- Whenever you cook, go ahead and wipe the counter and stove off after you are finished.
- Ever so often, take a minute to wipe the refrigerator down, inside and out. Also, take a minute here or there to look in there to see if any condiments need chucking.
- Every once in a while, grab some cleaner and clean the microwave, all of it, inside and out. Done—in a minute and a half.
- If the floor needs sweeping, grab the vac and clean it. If it needs mopping, move your rug and mop it clean.
- If the sink is looking grimy, spray a little cleaner with bleach on it, wait a few minutes and then using the spray nozzle, spray it out. Clean, done.
- Next!

The bedroom:
- Grab your hand-vac and vacuum all surfaces.
- Get the other upright vac and vacuum the carpet.

- Every week, strip the bed and wash the sheets.
- Check the mirrors occasionally and clean when necessary.

Repeat this process through every room in your house.

Things to do periodically:
- Go through all of your drawers and closet to see if you need to chuck anything.
- Maybe when you're putting up laundry, take one drawer, empty its contents and go through it. Take what you want to keep, fold it, put it up and take the other to the consignment or give it to charity. Takes no more than five minutes.
- As soon as you get your mail, sit down and go through all of it, chucking junk. Take the bills out of their envelopes and put it in your financial hub. Pay ASAP.

The point is to not wait until the house is covered in grime to do this. Do a little here and a little there and you will always, always have a clean house. Keep clutter under control and keep bills paid and your mind will be free!

Remember, procrastination is the enemy. Putting cleaning/de-cluttering off will only cause you more work later.

SOMETHING TO CONSIDER WHEN REPLACING CARPET

Whenever it's time to replace any carpeting in my house, I pull it up myself and my husband puts down laminate/wood flooring in its place. It's easier to put down than wood and stays cleaner than carpet. It also lasts a long time. Also, I don't have to strip or resurface it. And it's a *lot* less expensive.

Another great thing about this kind of flooring is that it stays so clean. I only have to mop it about once a month. If you decided to do this, remember, a lighter—oak—wood color will not show as much as a darker—cherry—wood color.

Of course, I do have to sweep/vacuum it about once a week. Other than that, it stays very clean. And it doesn't kill trees.

HERE'S HOW IT WORKS:
- Consider replacing carpet with laminate flooring.
- It stays very clean.
- A lighter color will show less dirt than a darker color.

THAT WASN'T SO BAD, WAS IT?

One of the biggest time-suckers, we all know, is house cleaning. But because none of us have won the lottery—yet, I'm still trying!—we have to do it ourselves.

But it's not so bad, is it?

Keep in mind that it may take you a year before you get your home straightened up. Invest the time to get it really clean even if it means doing most of it on weekends. As long as you do a little at a time, you can get there eventually. The point is to try and do it yourself. Stop fantasizing about fairies that will come in while you're at work and do it all for you.

So, just take your time and know that once your house is clean, if you take your thirty minutes a week, it will *stay* clean. No more worrying about when you're going to do it because you're only going to do it as it needs to be done and then when you have a spare minute or two.

And everyone has a spare minute or two, don't they? Yeah, and if you follow my plan, you'll have even more than that.